30th Infantry Division

Daniel D. Smith
MEMOIRS OF WORLD WAR II IN EUROPE
Co-authored by Dan Smith & Frank Barber

30th Infantry Division

Dan Smith
Honored WW2 Veteran

**Copyright 2013
Daniel D. Smith and Frank T. Barber**

QUOTE FROM TOM BROKAW'S BOOK
The Greatest Generation

"[The generation of World War 2 veterans] is, I believe, the greatest generation any society has ever produced."

"At a time in their lives when their days and nights should have been filled with innocent adventure, love, and the lessons of the workaday world, they were fighting in the most primitive conditions possible across the bloodied landscape of France, Belgium, Italy, Austria, and the coral islands of the Pacific. They answered the call to save the world from the two most powerful and ruthless military machines ever assembled, instruments of conquest in the hands of fascist maniacs. They faced great odds and a late start, but they did not protest. They succeeded on every front. They won the war; they saved the world. They came home to joyous and short-lived celebrations and immediately began the task of rebuilding their lives and the world they wanted. They married in record numbers and gave birth to another distinctive generation, the Baby Boomers. A grateful nation made it possible for more of them to attend college than any society had ever educated, anywhere. They gave the world new science, literature, art, industry, and economic strength unparalleled in the long curve of history. As they now reach the twilight of their adventurous and productive lives, they remain, for the most part, exceptionally modest. They have so many stories to tell, stories that in many cases they have never told before, because in a deep sense they didn't think that what they were doing was that special, because everyone else was doing it too."

The Greatest Generation,
Random House 2004
By Tom Brokaw

ABOUT THIS BOOK

The author, Dan Smith, is a personification of the World War II veterans that Tom Brokaw pays tribute to in his book, *The Greatest Generation,* quoted above.

Dan's gripping story demonstrates how Americans helped save the world in 1944 and 1945 in the European theater of the war, and how the American soldiers of the greatest generation helped set the stage for the unparalleled advances in science, literature, art, industry, and economic strength that occurred in the United States in the decades that followed.

CONTENTS

Chapter No.		Page No.
	Preface by Dan Smith	ix
1	*Life Before Going Overseas in World War II*	xiii
2	*England - Assembly of Troops and Materials For the 1944 Invasion of the Continent*	17
3	*Normandy - Landing on Omaha Beach and Battles Beyond*	25
4	*Northwestern France - The Chase from Mortain to the Seine*	37
5	*From Paris to the Siegfried Line*	45
6	*The Battle of the Bulge*	65
7	*Crossing the Roer River*	83
8	*Crossing the Rhine River*	97
9	*End of the War*	109
10	*Going Home*	129
	Time Table - Dan Smith's Service During World War II	143
	Table of Maps	151
	Table of Pictures	153
	Index	157

PREFACE BY DAN SMITH

People have asked me why I want this book to be written. It's a simple question, but the answer is not so simple.

God knows that there is a story to be told. I grew up as a teenager during the Great Depression of the 1930s. and then, when I had barely reached my early 20s, I was plunged into World War II, the greatest war of all time. I became a soldier in the U.S. Army's 30th Infantry Division, and was with the Division during the D-Day landings on the Normandy Beaches in June of 1944 and then for the next year during the 30th Division's year-long combat battle drive eastward and northward through France, Belgium, Holland and Germany until the end of the war in Europe came when we had reached the vicinity of Berlin in eastern Germany. It was a year-long period of unrelenting, day-to-day combat battle duty, and there are many stories to be told about what happened along the way.

When the war ended and I got back to the U.S., still alive, I don't remember that I had any urge to write about the stories. I was just glad to get back home alive and get on with my life, and there were a lot of other soldiers who had been through the war and were telling the stories. I do remember that I became known as a person who did not talk very much about my war experiences. I don't know why that was, either. Perhaps it was hereditary. My father had been in World War I and was also known for not talking about his war days.

I do know that during my entire life I have never begrudged the fact that it had been my lot to go through the Great Depression and World War II. I have always regarded them as valuable character-building experiences during which I learned priceless lessons of personal responsibility and discipline that helped me during the rest of my life.

I also know that, during the past five or ten years, I have begun to feel an urge to get my war experience stories down on paper. I don't know if I can explain the reason for this. Perhaps it's because, at age 91, time is running out. Perhaps it's because I'm getting some nudging from my family. Perhaps it's the fact that, with the advent of the Internet, there is a lot more information out there about the overall picture of the war in Europe, and it's now a lot easier to fit my pieces of the story into that overall picture and develop an understandable story of my own experiences. In any event, here I am, ready to publish the stories.

As I got into the business of working out each of the chapters in the story, I began to realize something that I had not been aware of before – namely, there are certain segments of the story in which I have an amazing detailed memory of what went on, and then there are other segments for which my memory is a total blank. Here again, I am not certain how to explain this. I can understand that the horrors of war, like death and injury, can possibly create memory blocks. My father and his family were in the undertaking business in the Chicago area, and so death was no stranger to me as I was growing up. However, in World War II there was mass destruction and death under circumstances that were totally new to me, and this could be the explanation. I'm sure the psychiatrists would have something to say about this. In any event, for those experiences where I have some memory block, I have adopted the practice of just telling all the available facts that I have surrounding the experience, and letting the readers assume what happened, if they so desire.

I want to acknowledge the help I have received in writing this book from my co-author, Frank Barber. Frank is my good friend whom I have known for over 70 years, starting with our bicycle riding days back in the 1940s. Frank is a lawyer and writes better than I do. The two of us worked together on this book, with me providing the facts that came out of my brain, and Frank using the facts to write the chapters and do the maps.

Fig. 1-The co-authors: Left to right: Frank Barber and Dan Smith

    I also want to acknowledge all the help and support I received from my family members, who monitored this whole thing constantly and made sure the ball was not dropped along the way. I especially want to acknowledge the help I received from my son, Michael Smith, who supervised this project and did the laborious job of scanning the wartime pictures from my albums and formatting them for inclusion in this book.

                                                       Daniel D. Smith
                                                       February 1, 2013

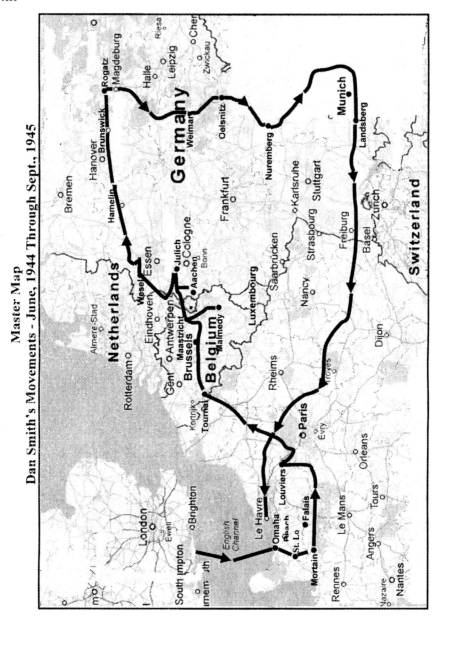

Master Map
Dan Smith's Movements - June, 1944 Through Sept., 1945

Chapter 1

LIFE BEFORE GOING OVERSEAS IN WORLD WAR II
Prior to February 1944

Map 1A
Life Before Going Overseas in World War II

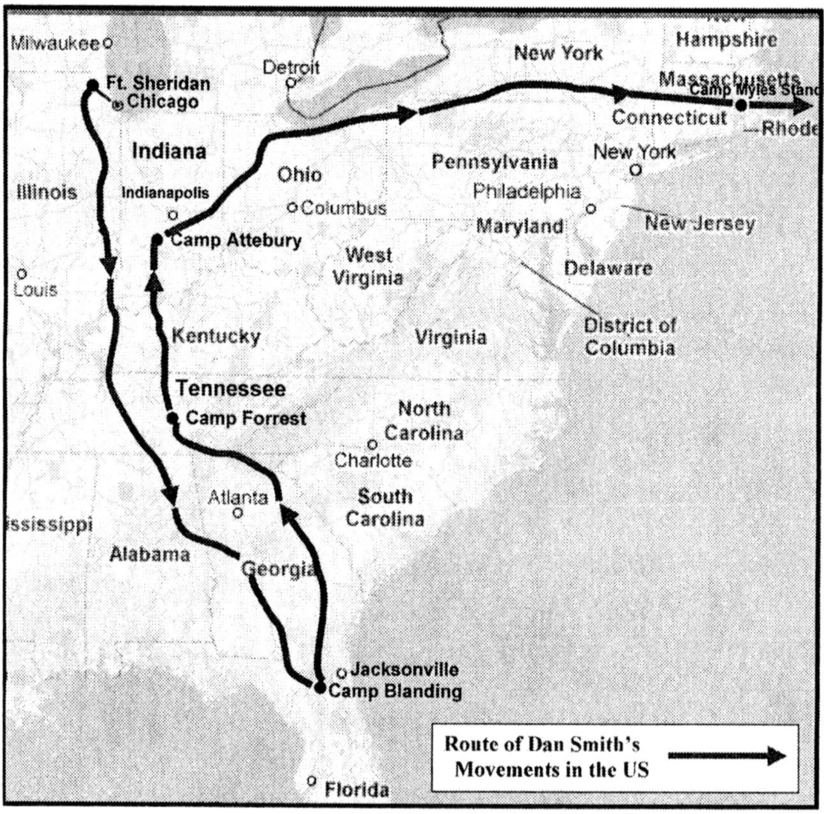

Chapter 1
LIFE BEFORE GOING OVERSEAS IN WORLD WAR II
Prior to February 1944

To start at the beginning, I was born in Oak Park, Illinois, a suburb of Chicago, in 1921, and attended St. Cornelius grade school there. My family moved to Chicago in 1927 and I graduated from Steinmetz High School in 1939 and then graduated from Wright Junior College in 1941.

My early years were filled with bicycling - both racing and otherwise. While I was still in grade school I had a heavy stock bicycle with balloon tires, and during my grade school and high school years, I did quite a bit of traveling on my bike in the countryside around Chicago. One time, I even road the 90 miles to Milwaukee, and then back.

During my first year at Wright Junior College, I received a circular from the Chicago Pedal Pushers (a Chicago bicycle club) advertising a 98 cent bargain ride to Aux Sable State Park south of Joliet, Illinois. The ride would be along the tow path to the locks on the Illinois-Michigan Canal. At the last minute, two of my friends and I decided to go, so we piled our bikes in my father's car and drove out. (My father was an undertaker, so there was plenty of room in the car.)

We had a swell time. But the trip taught me that my old balloon tire stock bike was not the right thing for long distance cycling. By a stroke of good fortune, my balloon tire bike was stolen just about then, and I ended up the proud possessor of a beautiful Schwinn New World bicycle, with thin tires and hand brakes, etc., etc.

With the new bike, I made my first long trip around Lake Michigan — up the east side of Lake Michigan to Muskegon, through the Straits, across the Peninsula, and then down through Green Bay and Milwaukee and back to Chicago.

During my two years at Wright Junior College, I did a lot of riding with various of the Chicago area social cycling clubs, all of whom were members of the Chicago Chapter of the League of American Wheelmen (LAW). I didn't join any one of the clubs, but I got to know a lot of the people who were involved in the LAW activities around Chicago. I came to know Harold Ade, who had been a member of the American Cycling Team that had competed in the 1932 Olympics races. Harold had settled in the Chicago area and had formed his own racing team, which competed in the many long-distance bicycle races that were held around Chicago and vicinity. Harold was in the process of forming also a social cycle club, which would be a member of the League of American Wheelmen and which included both boys and girls. He invited me to join this social club, which was known as the Oak Park Cycle Club, and I accepted. Of course, most of the boys in this club were also members of Harold's racing team, and I rode with them, and this was how I was introduced to bicycle *racing*.

Harold Ade expressed an interest in taking me on as a rookie member of his racing team, and I participated in a number of the training rides that his team took – *every day.* These rides told me that my Schwinn New World touring bike would not cut the mustard for racing, and in September 1941 I bought a BSA racing bike. The BSA was the favorite of racing riders. It had a steady grind, high gear ratio, no brakes, and was usually ridden with feet clamped to the pedals.

Still in 1941, Harold Ade arranged for me to compete as a rookie, along with three others of his rookies, in the Elgin to Chicago annual race. The race was 67 miles long, and started on a road that climbed up and over a ski slide mountain and then down into Chicago. As rookies, the four of us were allowed a five-minute head start on the real professionals in the race. I thought I was doing pretty good in the race. By the time I got up and over the mountain, my three other rookies were out of sight behind me and I rode alone for some time, until one of Harold Ade's professional team members caught up to me. I knew him of course, and we rode together for a while, until he took a fall. I stopped and helped him get back on his bike, and then we started out riding together again, this time, with me in the lead, breaking wind for him all the way down to near the finish line in Chicago. I was pretty bushed by this time, and it was then that he broke out around me and passed me and beat me to the finish line. He finished first and I finished second, a couple of minutes behind him. To this day, I believe that he faked the fall and took advantage of me on the rest of the race, but all I can do is chalk it up to a learning experience.

That night, at the dinner and festivities when the awards and trophies were handed out, I expected to receive a trophy for finishing second. I knew that trophies were awarded, because I had been in the homes of some of Harold's professional team members, and they had *closets* full of trophies. After the guy who beat me received his trophy, I went up for my turn, but was told that I did not get a trophy because I was a rookie and had been given a five-minute head start. Instead, they gave me a prize – namely, ***a stock bike with balloon tires!!!*** I can still remember my astonishment. I yelled out "What do you mean – a balloon tire bike?? I've already had a balloon tire bike. I don't need another one!!!" The humor of the whole thing overwhelmed me. It was like winning a watermelon eating contest and getting a watermelon for the prize.

Although I was tempted to quit bike racing at that point, I hung in for a few more races. Two weeks later, Harold Ade arranged for me to race in the Humboldt Park Bike Racing Bowl in Chicago. It was a huge bowl, and bike racers reached speeds of 60 mph going around in it. I didn't get a five-minute head start on this one, but I won it and received a nice gold medal, which I have to this day.

A couple of weeks later, Harold Ade put me in another race in the Chicago area. I don't remember the name of the race, but it was 45 miles long. It was a race I should not have entered. By this time I had given up the grueling training routine that racers must adhere to, and I went into the race fully unprepared. After the first half of the race, I was almost completely shot and I got off my bike, ready to turn around and go back home. But then something totally unexpected happened. All the riders in the race were riding in a single group that passed me and then, a few yards ahead of me they all plunged into a single crash. There were piles of bikes and riders all over the place. The race had come to a complete stop. I was the only one still standing. So I got back on my bike and forced myself to ride the rest of the miles in the race. Nobody passed me. I finished first and received a dandy trophy, one that I deserved much less than the one I didn't get in the Elgin to Chicago race.

That was the end of my racing career. I already knew that the racing life was not my cup of tea. I didn't want to be completely consumed by the unrelenting, day-to-day grueling training schedule. I also knew that I didn't want to continue in Harold Ade's social Oak Park Cycle Club, because the pressure on me in that club was to continue racing. In the meantime, I had become acquainted with the people in the Columbus Park Wheelmen, a League of American Wheelmen club that headquartered in the activities center in Columbus Park, located on the far west side of Chicago. Over the Labor Day Weekend in 1941, I joined a group of Columbus Park Wheelmen distance riders (John and Frank Dubnick, Frank Barber, and Phyllis Wiedman) for a weekend trip from Chicago to Milwaukee. We left Chicago late Saturday afternoon and stayed at a Youth Hostel near Rockford, Illinois, and then rode on to the Lake Geneva Youth Hostel the next day, and then on the following day rode on to Milwaukee and took the boat back to Chicago. It was the kind of bicycle riding that I enjoyed.

I joined the Columbus Park Wheelmen in the Spring of 1942 and found myself entering whole heartedly into the club's varying activities. I am still a member to this day. The club has stayed together for all the 72 years since it was formed. Time has taken its toll on the membership, and only about 15 of the original 35 members are still alive or able to attend the club reunions, and very little bicycle riding is now done. But we are a very close-knit group who will never forget the good times we have had together over all these years.

As everybody knows, World War II was declared on December 7, 1941, and in 1942 the boys in the Club began to get their draft notices. In July of 1942, as one final fling before entering the Armed Services, four of us club members (Frank and Johnny Dubnick, Frank Barber, and myself) decided to take a two-week bicycle trip from Chicago down through the chain of Youth Hostels through the picturesque Missouri Ozarks, south of St. Louis. At the time, I regarded this trip as the fitting climax to my cycling career.

Fig. 2 - At the start of the Ozarks Trip. Left to right: Frank Dubnick, John Dubnick, Dan Smith, Frank Barber

A book could be written about all the exciting and interesting experiences we had on this trip, but this is not the place for all of that. However, I would like to describe one breath-taking event that took place about halfway through our Ozarks trip, because it portends a similar experience that I had later on, at the end of my military service. We camped one night, out in the open, close to a railroad track, and I was having trouble getting to sleep, so I decided to take a walk. It was pitch dark, but I had my red baton flashlight with me, so I didn't have any trouble seeing my way. (All the boys in the bicycle club usually had these red batons, for use in directing traffic on our cycling events.) I started walking along the railroad tracks, thinking I might find a store that was still open, where I could get a soda or a candy bar. I didn't find one, but I did come to a road that crossed the tracks, and I discovered that there had been an automobile accident, and one of the cars had stalled on the tracks with locked gears. The drivers were getting excited because they knew that an express train was about to come down these tracks, so I ran back along the tracks in the direction from which the train was expected to come. I ran for over a mile and did indeed then see the train coming at me. I started waving my red baton frantically and, thank God, the engineer saw me and put on the brakes and everything else he could do to stop the train. It seemed like an eternity before the train actually stopped, but it did eventually screech to a stop and there was no crash. I thought I'd had enough excitement for the night, so I went back to our camp and went to bed. The automobile drivers and the engineer never did know who that stranger was who came out of nowhere and ran down the tracks with a red baton, and my three sleeping partners never did know whether to believe the story I told the next morning.

When we got back from the Ozarks, I started getting my affairs wound up and ready for me to go to war. My draft number came up in November, 1942, and on November 10th I went to the Army Enlistment Center in downtown Chicago and enlisted in the Army. Along with a lot of others new recruits, I was shipped in a truck up to Fort Sheridan, Illinois, just north of Chicago, and there I received my uniform and army equipment and all my shots. This was when Dan Smith, the cyclist, became Dan Smith, the soldier.

Fig. 3

As a Cyclist

Fig. 4

As a Soldier

Ch. 1 - Life Before Going Overseas

From Fort Sheridan, I moved to a number of different locations in the United States to get the kind of training needed for eventually crossing the Atlantic and entering World War II in Europe. This covered a period of over 15 months. To better visualize the location of the different training camps that I moved to, it is suggested that the reader refer to Map 1A which is included at the beginning of this chapter.

From Fort Sheridan, we were sent by train (in box cars) all the way down to Camp Blanding, Florida. It was a long distance, and the thought of riding all that way in box cars, with nothing to look at except the inside walls of the freight car, was not very appealing. However, in the beginning somebody asked me if I was any good at peeling potatoes, and fortunately I said yes, even though the thought of doing KP duty all the way down there was not very appealing either. It turned out to be a fortunate thing, because all of us KP guys who were peeling potatoes were in a separate box car, where we could open the side doors, and we sat in the opening, peeling potatoes and watching the beautiful countryside scenery go by – and we weren't working too hard at peeling the potatoes, either. I remember that many times along the way, we would have flocks of geese flying right alongside of us, and up close, hoping that we would drop some potatoes or other morsels.

Camp Blanding turned out to be an interesting place. Practically all the land in the vicinity of the camp was owned by the guy who owned the J.C. Penney Department Stores. On his land he built a whole community of cabins, and these served as a retirement community for retired J. C. Penney employees. They could retire from stores anywhere in the country and come down and live in this community for the rest of their lives.

At Camp Blanding we were assigned to the kind of duty we would expect to be doing for the rest of the war. Because my two years at Wright Junior College were in pre-med, the Army wanted to make a doctor out of me, but I said that I wanted something interesting. As a result, I found myself in the cavalry and reconnaissance and intelligence troop of the 30th Old Hickory

Infantry Division (Andrew Jackson's old Division). This was a very large troop because it served the entire 30th Division. During my stay at Camp Blanding I got to know a lot of the guys in this reconnaissance and intelligence troop. They were mostly from Tennessee, Kentucky and South Carolina. They were mountain folks. I was the only one with a degree, and I liked to rub it in, and they didn't like it very well. They were also mad at me because I would not go out with any of their sisters.

A lot of the officers in the 30th Division Reconnaissance and Intelligence Troop presented an interesting picture. Even though they would be riding around in jeeps, they liked to wear old cavalry uniforms and pretend that they were still in the cavalry, where the officers used to ride around on horses. Consequently, at the right front side of their jeeps they had spears (like the spears on cavalry horses), and at the left front side they had their guns mounted, so they could reach around with their right hand and grab the guns to fire back at the enemy, just like they were riding a horse. This throw-back stuff did not set too well with the Division commanders, and the throw-back officers were eventually told to cut it out and get modern.

While at Camp Blanding, we spent most of our time being trained in the use of the weaponry and vehicles and supplies of war. We attended classes and studied detailed manuals that had been prepared for us. These manuals were useful in our combat experiences when we eventually got into the war in Europe — but not always, especially when we were fighting in the hedgerows in Normandy, where the enemy never seemed to be operating like they were supposed to do, according to our manuals.

At Camp Blanding, I myself received intense training in the use and maintenance of 30- and 50-caliber machine guns, and I was certified as an instructor in these weapons and also as an anti-aircraft instructor As our training program progressed, and in all our combat experience later on in Europe, I was looked upon as the go-to guy when it came to operating, repairing and maintaining the machine guns. The same was true with respect to the high-powered scopes that we used in our reconnaissance activities and when we were directing artillery fire.

Our stay at Camp Blanding ended in May of 1943 when we moved to Tennessee to enter into field maneuvers. For this period of time our encampment area was at Camp Forrest, Tennessee, located near Tullahoma, Tennessee. The training was valuable, but there were times when the weather conditions and the surrounding mountainous terrain made operations almost impossible. Shortly after we arrived there, it rained for four days straight. The camp was wet and muddy, and when we tried to get out into the countryside for maneuvers we ran into washed out roads and missing bridges. One time, I was riding in a jeep with my driver, alongside another jeep, on the edge of one of these washouts when the bank gave away and our jeep slid all the way down into a deep ravine. We were not injured but the jeep was damaged and couldn't be moved, and we were way back in the woods, so we yelled up to the driver of the other jeep to go for help in getting us out. Well, on the way for help he himself rolled over and crushed his chest, and when they found him 24 hours later he was taken to a hospital. But he kept telling them that the two of us were still down in that ravine and needed help. They finally put together a search party and were able to find us. In the meantime, however, it appears that the word had gotten back to headquarters that we had been killed. The search party finally got us back to headquarters, and I spent the rest of the day walking around and startling people who thought I was dead.

After the weather improved, our 30th Division spent several months of intradivisional training to develop the skills necessary to carry out the "problems" that would be encountered in field maneuvers, and then, by September of 1943, we were ready to engage in a series of large-scale field maneuvers in which we were joined with four or five other Divisions. For a good part of the field maneuvers, our reconnaissance troops were assigned to take the role of the "enemy," and our jeeps were dressed up to look and sound like enemy tanks. We carried powder on board, which we exploded to sound like the guns from a tank. Sometimes, we actually used dynamite for this.

After two months of serious large-scale maneuvers, the decision was made that the desired training had been achieved, and, in November 1943, our 30th Division left Tennessee and moved by truck to Camp Attebury, Indiana, where we concentrated on preparation for movement overseas.

During our stay at Camp Attebury the Division Command came to the conclusion that the concept of a huge reconnaissance and intelligence troop that served the entire Division was too unwieldy and dangerous. The 30th Division had served in the war in Africa, using this concept, where the large-size Divisional recon and intelligence forces were fully armed and engaged in actual combat, rather than just reconnaissance. As a result of their role, they became targeted by the enemy, and large numbers in the troop were killed off. As a result of this experience, the Divisional Command made the decision to reduce the Divisional recon and intelligence force to a bare minimum, with no combat duties, and to spin off the main recon and intelligence function to newly formed recon and intelligence platoons in each of the many regiments in the Division.

As a result of this shift in policy, I found myself assigned to the Recon and Intelligence Platoon of the 117th Regiment. This was quite a comedown. Our 117th Regimental Recon and Intelligence Platoon contained only 20 men, with eight jeeps.

In this reorganization, most of my mountain folk friends from Tennessee, Kentucky and South Carolina were assigned to other regiments and I never saw them again. Just a couple of them happened to be assigned to the 117th Regiment with me. Most of the 20 guys in our platoon were now from New Jersey. They were good guys, and I got along with them just fine.

In February, 1944, after two months at Camp Attebury, our 30th Division moved by train to Camp Myles Standish, Massachusetts, one of the staging camps serving the Boston Port of Embarkation, where all of us got a whole new round of shots.

On February 12th our Division was loaded on three transport ships, the *John Ericsson,* the *Brazil* and the *Argentina,* and we left Boston Harbor in a blinding snowstorm as part of a convoy surrounded by Navy tankers and a huge number of other ships protecting us against enemy submarines. The weather was very bad for the whole crossing. Winter on the North Atlantic is very nasty.

The convoy was a spectacular sight, with ships spread out over the ocean as far as you could see. There was a battleship and countless destroyers patrolling around the edges. There was constant gunnery practice during the day and strict blackout during the night. There were a few rumors of submarine sightings, but nothing ever materialized, and, eventually we arrived in the Irish Sea and then split up for different destinations. Our 117th Regiment landed at Liverpool on February 22, 1944, and was then transported by rail to our staging area in the south of England, near London.

Our experiences in England, during the period leading up to the D-Day Normandy Beach landings in June, 1944, are described in the next Chapter.

Chapter 1 Pictures
from Dan Smith's Album

Fig. 5 - Dan Smith at Basic Training Camp in Florida

Fig. 6 - Training in the Use of Wartime Weaponry

Fig. 7 - Troop Ship in Boston Harbor, waiting for 30th Division to Embark.

Fig. 8 - 30th Division Troops on Board, Ready for Start of the Transit to England

Fig. 9 - Dan Smith on Board, Ready to start Transit to England

Chapter 2

ENGLAND
ASSEMBLY OF TROOPS AND MATERIALS FOR THE 1944 INVASION OF THE CONTINENT
February 1944 - June 1944

Map 2A
Assembly of Troops in England in Preparation for Normandy Landings

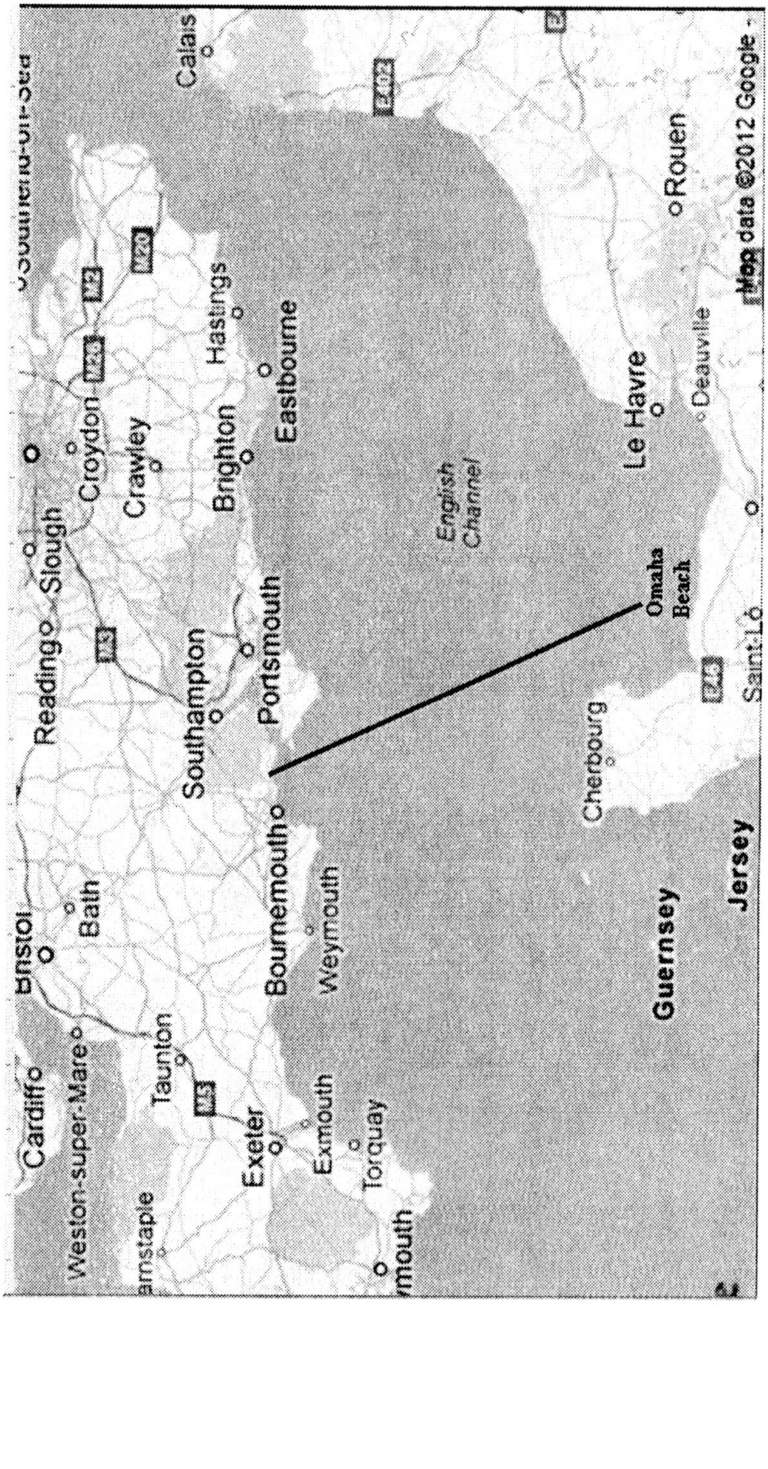

Chapter 2
ENGLAND
ASSEMBLY OF TROOPS AND MATERIALS FOR THE 1944 INVASION OF THE CONTINENT
February 1944 - June 1944

After crossing the North Atlantic and arriving in England in February of 1944, our 30th Division set up its encampments in the southern part of England, near London, and began preparations for crossing the English Channel to the beaches of Omaha Beach in France in the D-Day attack operations in June of 1944. Following this I was with the 30th Division on its combat drive against German forces and strongholds through France, Belgium, Holland and on into Germany, where our link-up was made with the Russian Army at Magdeburg, Germany, just west of Berlin, at the end of the war in April of 1945.

My memory is filled with the experiences we had during the preparation days in England, and the crossing to Omaha Beach, as well as the dangerous and exciting experiences that we had in the combat drive eastward and northward through Europe. The following is an account of some of my experiences and impressions at the very beginning – namely, the preparation and assembly days in England.

When the 30th Division sailed across the Atlantic and settled on the south coast of England, the soldiers of the Division knew that this was all for the purpose of a major invasion of Continental Europe, but we did not know when or where or how. We were only told that it would be "at some time in the future." Although there was some trepidation and fear among some of the troops as to what was to come, I remember many of the men, including myself, were excited and anxious to be a part of this great adventure.

Although we felt that we had been fully trained during our assignments back in the States, at Camp Blanding in Florida and Camp Forrest in Tennessee and Camp Atterbury in Indiana, we found that a primary purpose of the three or four months stay in England was much more intensified training and firing practice. The training periods were broken up with intervening periods of actually doing nothing, and the boredom and tediousness of all this for so many months began to be a burden, so we began to look for ways of relieving the boredom by getting familiar with England and the English people and their ways of living. Most of us had never been to England before.

We found excuses for having special dinners, playing volleyball, and attending special shows and movies that were brought in. At one point, we were given passes to go to London and see the sights. I myself took advantage of this. I remember that on one occasion when I went to London, I was walking the streets seeing the sights and just talking to friendly English people. One Englishman that I met asked me, "What would you like to do?" and I answered, "I would like to get a good meal." So he took me to a hotel, which had been knocked down by the bombing, but which still had a restaurant in the basement. The dinner I had there was memorable. It was a three-course meal, including a wine which was very good.

On my London pass, I was able to do other things. I visited an immense museum, which seemed to be built entirely of glass. (I wonder if it ever survived subsequent bombings.) I also went to see a play in a theater, and, although I don't remember too much about the play, the interesting and amusing thing that I do recall was that one of the actors was an Englishman who was trying to play the part of an American with an American accent.

Another thing I remember is that, in my trips, such as the trip to London, I usually went alone. None of the other guys seemed to want to do the things that I wanted. They were not interested in museums or theaters or fancy restaurants. All they wanted to do was to get a girl, and the girls seemed to be very receptive. At that time, after four years of war, there were very few English men left in England. They were somewhere in Europe, fighting the war, and many, many had been killed. The girls were left behind, and when American soldiers appeared, the girls were very good at suggesting things to do. They mainly wanted men, chocolates and chewing gum.

With the shortage of men, a lot of the jobs, big and small, were left to the women. Given my interest in cycling, I was particularly intrigued with the fact that the English corps of messengers was made up entirely of girls riding bicycles. The messenger girls were noted for how fast and recklessly they rode in order to get the messages through. I actually witnessed more than one incident where one of the girls got going so fast that she missed a turn in the road and slid out of control into the roadside shrubbery. None of them got hurt.

When we were bivouacked in various locations out in the English countryside, we had opportunity to get acquainted with English people who lived in countryside houses. It was interesting to note that most of the homes had barns, which originally were stables, and in each of the barns was a car (which was rarely used because of gas restraints). It was also interesting to see that many of the barns were under construction, because there was a movement at this time in England to convert barns such as these to somewhat elite, fancy two-story houses (or, in modern language, condos).

Our time in the rural areas also allowed us to visit some of the small pubs that were everywhere. On my first visit to a pub, the thing that stood out for me was the fact that the beer I was given at first tasted more like iced tea than beer.

Sometimes, to relieve the tension and boredom, we resorted to practical jokes on one another. One time, as we were moving our location from one encampment to another, in a parade of jeeps and trucks, we made a rest stop at a small community that had a novelty shop. In the shop, I saw a pair of girls panties hanging on a rack, and they were so unbelievably cheap that I had to buy them. I took them out and hung them over the steering wheel of the truck we were riding in, and everybody got a good laugh. We next saw them draped over the entrance flap of the Major's tent in the morning when we camped overnight on the trip. And we next saw them hanging on the rear end of the Major's jeep as he led the parade to the next encampment. The Major never caught on, but the men had a chance to laugh quite a bit. (On closer searching of my memory, I am now a little uncertain as to whether this incident occurred in England, or previously back in the United States – but, what the heck.)

We found that the English people themselves were able to maintain their sense of humor, in spite of being under seige for such a long time. One of the guys in our Regiment, who was a golfer, found some time to go visit a golf course which was on the outskirts of London. He didn't play golf, but he came back laughing because he had been in the Pro Shop of the Golf Club (the Richmond Golf Club) and had picked up a copy of the rules of play that were then in effect. The rules read as follows:

RICHMOND GOLF CLUB
TEMPORARY RULES. 1940

1. Players are asked to collect Bomb and Shrapnel splinters to save these causing damage to the Mowing Machines

2. In Competitions, during gunfire or while bombs are falling, players may take cover without penalty for ceasing play.

3. The positions of known delayed action bombs are marked by red flags at reasonably but not guaranteed, safe distance therefrom.

4. Shrapnel and/or bomb splinters on the Fairways, or in Bunkers within a club's length of a ball, may be moved without penalty, and no penalty shall be incurred if a ball is thereby caused to move accidentally.

5. A ball moved by enemy action may be replaced, or if lost or destroyed, a ball may be dropped not nearer the hole without penalty.

6. A ball lying in a crater may be lifted and dropped, not nearer the hole, preserving the line to the hole, without penalty.

7. A player whose stroke is affected by the simultaneous explosion of a bomb may play another ball from the same place. Penalty one stroke.

When our quarters were being moved closer to the water as the time for the invasion approached, we had opportunity to observe

Ch. 2 - Assembly of Troops in England

the English people and the waterfront cities and their wharves. The wharves turned out to be the daily gathering place for retired citizens. In a waterfront city, the retiring citizens are mostly formerly seafaring men, who spent most of their lives on the ocean. They are uniquely identifiable by the texture of the skin on their faces, testifying to the effect of the salty winds and sprays to which they have been exposed.

The retirees on the wharves were outstanding story tellers. Their tales of the adventures they'd had in decades after decades at sea are fascinating, and they never run out of them. I have noticed that the ladies who join the men are even better at telling the tales than the men.

Near the end of our stay, some of us were able to take a side trip over to Wales, which seemed to us to be a completely foreign land. The Welsh have their own language, which was entirely foreign and needed translation for all of us who spoke only English. The countryside was sprinkled with Roman Baths, and people were actually in there swimming. I was given the opportunity to do so, but declined.

At the very end of our stay in England, we were stationed in the marshalling areas near the city of Southampton, and had a view of the fine harbor where the great ocean liners, in times of peace, sat at the docks. Now there was nothing to be seen but the boats of our fleet and the English fleet.

At the very end also, we were given a supply of putty and ordered to "waterproof" our jeeps, so they would not stall when they were driven off the transport boats in several feet of water during the upcoming landings on the Normandy beaches. Since I appeared to be more mechanically inclined than some of the other men, I found myself doing a "waterproofing" job on quite a few jeeps other than my own. "Waterproofing" involved using the putty to seal all cracks and openings, sealing the ignition systems, and placing extensions on intake and exhaust pipes, so they would extend up along the windshields to provide outlets above the jeep.

Finally, on June 9 (D-Day + 3), our 117th Infantry Regiment loaded into transport boats near Southampton and set out across the

English Channel for Omaha Beach in Normandy, France.. We arrived at a position offshore of Omaha Beach the morning of June 10 (D-Day + 4).

The story of our landing and our experiences on the Beach and in Normandy and beyond will be the subject of subsequent chapters.

Chapter 3

NORMANDY
LANDING ON OMAHA BEACH AND THE BATTLES BEYOND
June 1944 - August 1944

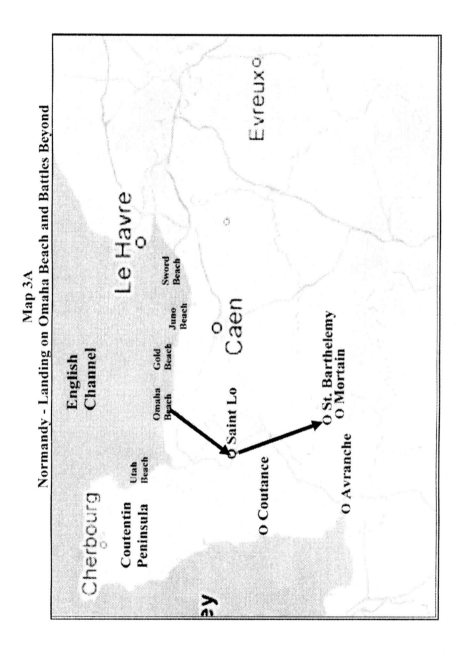

Map 3A
Normandy - Landing on Omaha Beach and Battles Beyond

Chapter 3

NORMANDY
LANDING ON OMAHA BEACH AND THE BATTLES BEYOND
June 1944 - August 1944

The landing on Omaha Beach, Normandy, was full of experiences that I will never forget. The transport boats which carried our 30th Division across the English Channel arrived at an offshore position at Omaha Beach on June 10th, 1944, and the unloading began.

The first landings at Omaha Beach had been made four days earlier by the 29th Division, and the Germans had thrown everything they had, from land and from the air and from the water, against these landings. As we approached, we could see the hulks of many ships, both Allied and enemy, that had been sunk.

In our landing operation, our transport boats came in as close to shore as they could and then unloaded men and supplies and vehicles onto barges, which then got us to a point near the shore where the water was only two to four feet deep. All the men waded ashore, and the jeeps and trucks and other vehicles were driven off the barge and into the water and up onto the beach.

The vehicles which had been properly waterproofed made it onto the beach very handily, but quite a few of those that had not been readied stalled out and were left stranded.

Looking back now, it seems a little hard to believe, but I remember that most of us were in high spirits when we were landing and actually found humor in some of the things that happened. I laughed so hard at our Colonel climbing down the rope ladder onto the barge that my helmet fell off and floated away. However, when we actually got on the beach the sheer devastation that we saw brought us back to reality.

The beach and the cliffs beyond it were all torn to hell by the terrific battle that had gone on there. The beach was cluttered with burned out jeeps and tanks and trucks and knocked out pill boxes.

At points along the beach there were collections of bodies of American soldiers waiting to be taken back to England. We had an overwhelming feeling of gratitude for what the 29th Division had sacrificed for us. Their Division was decimated, and I'm not sure the few survivors were ever able to get back into action.

During all of this, I was amazed that there was no sign of any defensive action being taken by the Germans against us. There were no German naval vessels, no attacks from the air, and no counterattacks from the beach or the cliffs or the surrounding land. It would have been a beautiful opportunity for Goering to deal us a heavy blow, but apparently he had used up all his defensive resources against the first landings — another reason for our gratitude to the 29th Division.

On the beach, amidst all the clutter, there were many 29th Division helmets. I picked one up to replace the one I had lost, and inside this I put a nice leather liner that I had found in a German helmet, so I had my own custom-made helmet.

As soon as possible, we climbed our way up the 1,000 foot cliff, and, after moving a mile or two inland past ruined buildings, we immediately found ourselves in the Normandy terrain, consisting of miles and miles of small farms, separated by mounds of hedgerows, where the defensive forces of the German Army were securely established and where the American troops of General Omar Bradley's First Army who had preceded us were engaged in fierce battle with the Germans.

Before proceeding with the account of my own personal experiences starting at this point, it will be well to pause and provide some background by describing the overall picture of the Allied Forces Invasion status at the time we entered into it, four days after it began. To understand this background description it is suggested that the reader refer to Map 3-A which is included at the beginning of this chapter. Map 3-A shows the location of the various northern Normandy towns and battlegrounds that are described in this chapter.

The Allied Invasion which started on June 6, 1944, involved landing of Allied troops at five different beaches on the Normandy

Ch. 3 - Landing on Normandy Beaches and Battles Beyond

northern coast. These beaches, starting from west to east, were Utah Beach, Omaha Beach, Gold Beach, Juno Beach, and Sword Beach. General Omar Bradley's First Army forces landed on Utah and Omaha, and the British and Canadian forces under Field General Montgomery landed on Gold, Juno and Sword.

Upon landing and securing the Utah and Omaha beaches, General Bradley's First Army moved a few miles to the south, to set up an advancing front line stretching for about 50 miles from west to east along a line just south of the northern Normandy coastline. Field General Montgomery's combined British and Canadian forces set up a similar front line, intended for advancing in the direction of Caen in the northeastern part of Normandy.

General Bradley's initial and very important objective for his First Army was actually to move toward the western coastline of France (through Normandy and Brittany) in order to capture as many western coastal seaports as possible. This was considered crucial because great numbers of supply and troop ships were arriving from the US, and they needed seaports that would allow the ocean-going ships to dock and unload their cargos and men. The northern Normandy beaches were not adapted to receive such ships, especially in bad weather, and American control of seaports (such as Cherbourg, Coutance, Avranche, and Brest) was a necessary objective.

In view of this objective, the First Army troops who had landed at Utah Beach quickly began moving up the Cotentin Peninsula and, on June 27th, after stiff fighting, forced the surrender of the major port of Cherbourg, located at the northern tip of the Peninsula. Cherbourg was an especially valuable prize because it was not only a major shipping port but also an important German submarine base. However, the value of this capture was somewhat diminished because, before its capture, German engineers completely demolished the port and all its facilities and ensured that it would take many months before it was ready to receive any supply or troop ships from the US. However, at least the submarine base was demolished and rendered inoperative.

This left General Bradley with the still important mission of driving through the Normandy and Brittany battlefield to capture the seaports on the western coast of France. The westerly flank of his battle front line was still occupied with securing gains made on the Cotentin Peninsula and in Cherbourg, so he used the middle and easterly flanks of his First Army to push southward to Saint Lo, an important crossroad city that controlled the roads leading to the western French coastline.

This movement proved to be very slow and costly, for a number of reasons. A key terrain obstacle was the Normandy hedgerow country itself. Normandy farmers traditionally enclosed their farms with thick hedgerows. These hedgerows began right behind the original First Army landing beaches and extended up to 50 miles inland in some areas. They couldn't have made a more effective defense obstacle if they had intentionally been designed for that purpose. They also made excellent defense positions, providing cover and concealment for the enemy defenders. Finally, the hedgerows restricted observation, making the effective use of artillery and tank guns almost impossible.

Like the terrain, the weather also affected Bradley's operations in Normandy. Constant rain during June and July hampered the efforts of the First Army. The early summer of 1944 was the worst since 1900. The marshlands of Normandy turned into muddy swamps.

In spite of these obstacles, the First Army made progress toward Saint Lo, but then another obstacle arose, in the form of a major counterattack mounted by the German Armed Forces, moving from the eastern part of Normandy. This was a two-pronged attack, one column directed at the city of Saint Lo, and another column directed at Mortain, a city about 40 miles south of Saint Lo. The main objective of this counterattack was to drive a wedge all the way to the west coast of France, and thus isolate and capture all of the First Army troops north of this wedge, and thus thwart the First Army's attempt to capture seaports on the west coast. In order to make this counterattack, it was necessary for the German high command to pull forces away from General Montgomery's

Ch. 3 - Landing on Normandy Beaches and Battles Beyond   31

advancing British and Canadian forces in the Caen area, and this was beneficial to the Allied cause, but of course the counterattack increased the difficulties that the American First Army was having in the attack on Saint Lo.

General Bradley's southbound First Army arrived at Saint Lo at about the time the northern column of the German counterattack arrived there, and there was devastating warfare in and around that city for several weeks. Saint Lo finally was captured by the First Army on July 18th, but the city remained under enemy fire, and the First Army's attempt to move beyond the city toward the French coastline had ground to a stalemate. An element of the First Army was ordered to go around Saint Lo and proceed further south to defend against the southern column of the German counterattack at Mortain.

While all of this was going on, General Patton was in England, assembling a new army, named the Third Army, whose objective was to cross the English Channel and land on Normandy beaches and proceed southward down through Saint Lo and then turn westward toward the western French coast, to assist in the still important objective of capturing French seaports. The Third Army had in fact crossed the English Channel and was assembling at a point just north of Saint Lo and was becoming operational. However, the stalemate at Saint Lo impeded its progress.

Even further, while all of this was going on, General Eisenhower was developing plans for an additional super-offensive movement, given the code name Cobra, designed to supplement and effectuate the American forces' drive toward the western French Coast. Operation Cobra was actually launched at the stalemated Saint Lo area on about July 25th. It consisted of a concentrated aerial bombardment from thousands of Allied aircraft, combined with an intensified ground attack by the First Army. It succeeded in breaking the stalemate and creating a corridor for Bradley's First Army and Patton's 3rd Army to break through and proceed onward toward their respective goals on the western coast of France.

Quickly following this, the First Army elements that had been sent down to Mortain, combined with effective rocket bombing from the English aerial rocket attack, succeeded in turning back the German counteroffensive at this point.

These two Allied victories then revealed another element of the war that had not been readily apparent to them before. It brought to light the fact that the German forces in the Normandy front had become so weak and tired and worn out and undermanned that they were in collapse and unable to continue. The breakthrough at Saint Lo and the collapse of the German counterattack at the bloody battlegrounds of Mortain convinced the German High Command that they had no option other than to abandon the German defense of Normandy and retreat back to Germany.

The disintegration of the German forces at Saint Lo and Mortain has been described as the turning point of the war in Europe. After this, the character of the war changed completely. The Armed Forces' objective suddenly became that of "chasing the Germans back to Berlin." The matter of driving westward toward the French seaports was no longer pertinent. With the battle grounds rapidly retreating eastward and northward toward Germany, the French seaports on the western coast were becoming too far away from the action to be effective, and the incoming US supply and troop ships were looking for closer seaports such as LeHavre and Antwerp, the best port in Europe. Bradley's First Army and Patton's Third Army were free to abandon their drive toward France's west coast and to join the chase of the retreating German Armies.

With the benefit of all the foregoing background information, it is time now for me to resume description of the experiences that I encountered after landing on Omaha Beach and climbing the cliffs to arrive at the heavily defended Normandy hedgerow terrain.

Our 30th Division was assigned to General Bradley's First Army, which at that time was slowly making its way south in the direction of Saint Lo. I found myself in a reconnaissance regimental patrol, a subdivision of the 30th Division. We had seven jeeps, two mounting 50 caliber machine guns, three of the 30 caliber machine guns, four radios, and 20 men.

The road toward Saint Lo went through heavily defended hedgerow country. Our platoon's job was to scout ahead of our

Ch. 3 - Landing on Normandy Beaches and Battles Beyond

regimental forces, and then report back to the regiment with information on the status of the road ahead. We made 12 such nightly patrols before our lieutenant and radio man were shot from enemy fire from behind the hedgerows. At one point, just after we had crossed the Vire River on July 7th, some Germans raced tanks straight down the road and got between our patrol and our headquarters. Our regiment engaged them with a counterattack. There were bullets everywhere. I made it over a hedgerow (I'll never know how) and took cover in a small hole. I had part of one foot hanging out the hole, and the Germans fired at it for 20 minutes and then left. I then ran through the fields back to our headquarters. In jumping over the hedge row, I landed on my rifle actuator and drove it into my hand. When I pulled my hand back, all the meat came off too. Back at headquarters, the Colonel saw me and stopped the counterattack. A major, who was a doctor, patched me up with my first aid kit. I learned that the Sulfa powder in those kits didn't work. The hand took three weeks to heal.

On July 12th, while we were still making our way toward Saint Lo, our 30th Division was designated as the lead unit in Operation Cobra, whose mission was to spearhead the breakthrough at Saint Lo, thus providing a corridor allowing Bradley's First Army and Patton's Third Army to proceed southward and westward to the French western coast.

When our Regiment had almost reached Saint Lo, where everything was in a stalemate, and at a point when operation Cobra and its heavy aerial bombardment from Allied aircraft was about to be launched, a fleet of American P24s took a wrong turn and bombarded our own forces while we were out in the road to Saint Lo. It was a tragic mistake. Our platoon was holding a weak place between Divisions. We were in a small sunken dip in the road. I saw the attack coming. The P24s were coming at a right angle to our line. I asked somebody, "What are all those black specks in the sky?" They turned out to be the bombs. They rained down on a field, jumped the road and hit the field in front of us. I was lifted three feet from my seat. Many cattle were hit, but none of them seemed to fall. In our Regiment a man we had left at headquarters as a map-maker was killed. A general, a reporter and our chaplain died at regimental headquarters. Many other units were badly cut up. I saw my first casualty, I believe, in D Company. I saw shoes in trees with feet in them. I did not know how many casualties there were, but I later heard that this "friendly fire" killed 25 men and wounded 131 of us.

And then, as the unbelievable part of this story, ***the same thing happened again the next day.*** This second erroneous attack from our own planes killed 111 men, including Lieutenant General Leslie McNair, and wounded 490. Never again did our tank battalion camouflage their tanks. Instead, they put on bright red, green and orange panels.

At any rate, Operation Cobra was launched the next day, and the combination of the concentrated Allied aerial attack and the renewed ground attacks from U.S. forces did indeed succeed in breaking the stalemate at Saint Lo and allowed General Bradley's First Army and General Patton's Third Army to break through and continue their drive toward the western coast of France.

Our Regiment did not try to enter Saint Lo. Instead, we were ordered to by-pass it and proceed southward for 40 miles to support the Allied troops which were attempting to capture the town of Mortain and ward off the counterattack which the Germans had launched in the southern prong of their drive toward the western coast of France.

We actually never got to Mortain. When we arrived in St. Barthelemy, a small town just a few miles north of Mortain, we found ourselves surrounded by German forces. The town of Mortain was held by German troops, and these troops were being reinforced by the German counterattack troops coming from the east. Our First Army troops which were attempting to capture Mortain found themselves surrounded by the enemy. Several units of a U.S. Infantry had been assigned to protect an important hill ("Hill 314"), and these units had themselves been surrounded by the enemy and were in danger of being annihilated. Several books have been written about the battle of Hill 314.

Ch. 3 - Landing on Normandy Beaches and Battles Beyond

The warfare in the Mortain/St. Barthelemy area continued for a whole week, with the Germans using four armored divisions. The town of Mortain was leveled. The forest around it was cut down to stumps. Many U.S. troops were surrounded and about 200 were captured. One night the Germans returned the worst of our wounded. In the course of the battle the Germans sent in 100 tanks against us and captured all of our antitank guns and used them against us. We were running out of supplies, and US air force planes attempted to help us out with air drops. The situation was looking very bleak.

Some relief appeared at the end when a battalion of U.S. antitank vehicles caught up to us at St. Barthelemy, and started making good progress at turning the German tank attacks back. And then, as the crowning point, the battle of Mortain was finally won by the Allies when fleets of English Typhoons (large armored aircraft) arrived and started firing rockets at the German positions throughout the Mortain/St. Barthelemy area. What a racket these rockets made!! We didn't know there was such a thing as a rocket. We were told that the Typhoons got 73 tanks in one hour. What a road block this caused. When we went out on patrol the next morning, all the demolished German tanks were there, but there were no German soldiers, just bodies. The Germans did manage to salvage a lot of stuff off the tanks, however, even the guns.

The battle of Mortain had definitely been won by the Allies. We were given the official word that, in view of the Allied victories at the two key points (Saint Lo and Mortain), the German High Command had made the decision to abandon Normandy and the rest of France to the Allies and to retreat back to Germany.

The orders given to our 30th Division and to all the other Allied troops in the area were to discontinue the drive toward the western seacoast ports of France and to put all our efforts toward "Chasing the Germans back to Germany."

The start of the chase to Germany will be the subject of the next Chapter.

Chapter 4

NORTHWESTERN FRANCE
THE CHASE FROM MORTAIN TO THE SEINE
August 1944

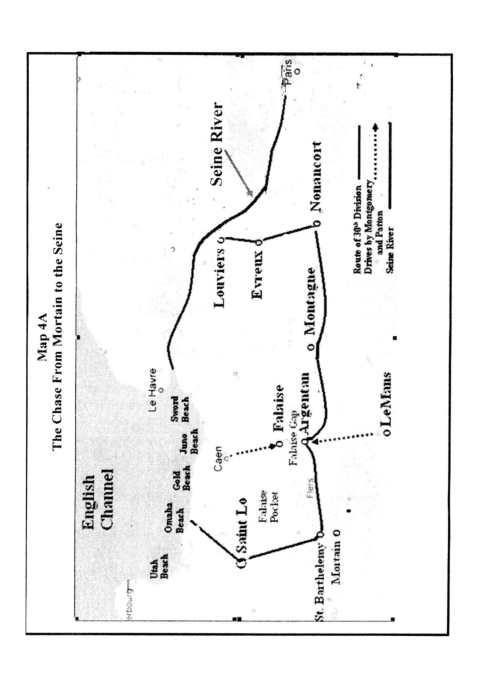

Chapter 4

NORTHWESTERN FRANCE
THE CHASE FROM MORTAIN TO THE SEINE
August 1944

When the German counterattack was stopped both at Saint Lo and Mortain, we got intelligence reports that the Germans had made the decision to abandon its defense efforts in Normandy and retreat back to Germany. Our Division got the word that our mission now was to follow them in their retreat and to push them as fast as possible by engaging their rear echelons and keeping them off balance as they fled.

My part of this operation was as part of an 18-man Recon patrol group, a part of the 117th Reconnaissance Regiment. The daily mission of our patrol group was to go out 23 miles ahead of our regimental battle line, and get as close as safely possible to the rear flanks of the retreating enemy, and to get as much possible information back to regimental headquarter as we could gather about the location of the enemy troops, supplies, vehicles, and armament. This was done by radio. Our mission was strictly to gather information, and we were not to engage the enemy in battle. Our groups traveled in jeeps, equipped with machine guns, scopes and radio.

This was the mode of operation of our patrol group, starting out from Mortain and continuing all the way across France, Belgium, Netherlands and Germany, until the end of the war almost a year later when we had arrived in Magdeburg, Germany. We would start each day by going out the 23 miles ahead of our regimental battle line and carrying out our reconnaissance duties during the day and then returning to our advancing regimental headquarters at the end of the day. The 23 miles was chosen because our regimental troops had to walk and this was about the distance that a regiment could walk in one day. On days when troop trucks or other vehicles were available, the distance covered by the regiment in a day could be as much as 100 or 200 miles. However, those non-walking days were not too frequent, because, like all other supplies and equipment, trucks were in short supply.

The instructions that our recon patrol operated under sometimes led to some unique experiences. There were times when some of the retreating Germans would deliberately fall behind their rear lines and seek out our patrol and try to surrender to us. We never tried to take any of these as prisoners. We would just send them back toward our advancing headquarters where the formal capture could be made to Regimental officers.

There were other times when the retreating Germans would see us and try to engage our patrol in battle by firing at us. They wanted us to fire back at them because this would allow them to locate our position more accurately, so they could knock us out. We never fired back. On some rare occasions we would fire at a barn or haystack to set it on fire to distract them, but in those cases we would fire without tracers. As time went on, the Germans developed a strategy of deploying gun positions out of sight to the right and/or left of the center line in which our patrol group was advancing — their plan being to let us drive into the center of this trap and then close in on us from the left and the right to make the kill. Our biggest effort was to maintain a close watch for these right and left traps.

In the very beginning of our chase of the Germans in their retreat, we were making fairly good progress. After leaving our starting position, in the Mortain/St. Barthelemy area, we quickly went through the town of Flers and then on toward the town of Falaise. This is where we ran into the middle of an intense situation that was developing – namely, the setting of the Falaise Pocket or Trap.

Here again, it will be well to pause and take time to provide some background showing the status of the Allied Forces Invasion operations at this point, and to describe the developments and the opportunity that led the Allied Command to decide to create the Falaise Pocket, a huge maneuver designed to trap and capture or

Ch. 4 – The Chase from Mortain to the Seine

destroy 80,000 to 100,000 of Germany's crack troops. To understand this background description it is suggested that the reader refer to Map 4A which is included at the beginning of this chapter. Map 4A shows the location of the various northern Normandy towns and battlegrounds that are about to be described.

In order to make the two-pronged German counter attack against Saint Lo and Mortain, as described in the previous chapter, it was necessary for the German command to borrow a significant number of crack German troops from the area around Caen where they were defending against Field Marshal Montgomery's British and Canadian forces who were driving southward and eastward from the Gold, Juno and Sword beaches. This German weakness around the Caen area allowed Montgomery's forces to make significant progress. By the time the battles at Saint Lo and Mortain had been won by the US forces, Montgomery's armies had captured Caen and were poised to continue their drive eastward toward Paris.

In the meantime, when the American's successful Operation Cobra attack broke the stalemate at Saint Lo and opened the corridor for the US First and Third Armies to continue their missions to the west and south, General Patton's Third Army quickly swept southward and westward through Brittany and then turned eastward in its drive toward Paris. By the time the battle at Mortain had been won, Patton's forces had captured the city of LeMans, and they too were poised to drive eastward on to Paris.

At the same time, the crack German forces who had lost the battles of Saint Lo and Mortain were standing still, attempting to decide their next strategy. Hitler himself wanted them to regroup and continue the counterattack westward to the coast. His generals at the scene were telling him that they did not have the resources to do this. This indecision cost the Germans a valuable amount of time, and, by the time they finally made the decision to give up the counterattacks and start their retreat back to Germany, the Allied High Command recognized that they had a rare opportunity to catch all those Germans in a pocket where they and their equipment could be killed or captured and obliterated from the scene. This they could do by having Montgomery's troops turn south and Patton's troops turn north and meet somewhere near Falaise to create the pocket.

The American High Command gave the order to proceed with this plan and, indeed, within about a week, Montgomery's forces had arrived at Falaise and Patton's forces had arrived at Argentan, leaving still a gap of about 12 miles, which was referred to as the Falaise Gap. At this time, in a decision which has been extensively debated in the history books, the American High Command decided to hold back and not to try immediately to close this gap, apparently fearing that they did not have enough power to maintain the closure, and also fearing that there would be too much risk of Montgomery's and Patton's forces endangering each other with friendly fire. After about a week, when Allied forces had been more firmly built up, the gap was finally closed. However, during this time a significant number of German troops were able to escape through the gap. Although these troops had to leave all their arms and equipment behind them, they were nevertheless then available to be reorganized and rearmed in time to slow the subsequent Allied advance into Belgium, Netherlands and Germany.

However, in spite of the fact that substantial numbers of Germans had escaped through the gap, nevertheless the Germans suffered massive losses in the Falaise operation. Estimates suggest that 80,000 to 100,000 thousand German troops were caught in the pocket, of which 10,000 to 15,000 were killed, 40,000 to 50,000 taken prisoner, and 20,000 to 50,000 escaped. In the pocket, the Germans lost 94% of their armour, nearly all of their artillery, and 70% of their vehicles.

With the benefit of the foregoing background information, it is time now for me to resume description of the experiences that our regiment encountered as we approached the town of Falaise in our chase of the Germans.

As mentioned, we arrived in the Falais area just as the Gap was finally being closed. Although some elements of our 30th Division assisted General Patton's Third Army in closing the Gap, our 117th Regiment passed on through the area in our drive to the Seine River. We did have one rather amusing experience in the area, however, when we came across a tank bearing the name "Tea Time." I asked the name of their unit and was told "Her Majesty's Household Cavalry." We called this information in to Headquarters, and the radio man said "That was a joke, wasn't it?" The famous Household Cavalry can usually be seen at Buckingham Palace. Apparently the Tea Time tank was a part of Montgomery's British forces and had come south through the Gap before it was finally closed.

After passing through the Falaise area we continued our standard practice of moving forward, with our 18 man reconnaissance patrol starting out each day by jeeping 23 miles ahead and then waiting for the regiment to catch up. We proceeded in a line that dipped south and east toward the town of Montagne. My memory of this leg of our journey is that the roads and the terrain were very dusty. The dust in our eyes was terrible. We could hardly see the vehicle in front of us, and when the two little red lights in the jeep ahead of us turned vertical, we stopped.

As we got to the vicinity of Montagne, we ran out of gas and had to lay low for two or three days. We had to stay in houses, and we saw our first civilians in nearly two months. There were none in the previous combat areas. The civilian people really welcomed us, and it was a pleasant experience, but we couldn't linger because it was our job to get to the Seine River.

Following our delay at Montagne, we resumed the same daily operation toward the east, with our patrol 23 miles out ahead of the main line during the day, and then dropping back to headquarters at night. There was only sporadic resistance along this stretch. We reached the town of Nonancourt, where there was no resistance from the enemy, and then made a turn to the north, toward Evreux.

The town of Evreux was the site of a major military airfield, used by the Luftwaffe earlier in the war. When we arrived there the area had been abandoned by the Germans, and on about August 23rd we occupied the town without any resistance.

At Evreux, we were held while the Allied High Command made their decision as to how the occupation of Paris was to be made. The German resistance at the Seine River had practically disappeared, and Paris was available to be formally occupied. For political and diplomatic reasons, the Allied decision was finally made that General DeGaulle's newly formed Free French Army, together with a single Allied Forces division (the American 4th Division) would have the honor of entering and "occupying" Paris. All the other Allied forces that were in the vicinity would bypass Paris and cross the Seine at various spots to the west of Paris.

Our regiment originally was given the order to proceed north from Evreux and make the crossing at the town of Louviers. From our positions in Evreux and Louviers we were close enough to see the Eiffel Tower, although to the best of my memory I was so busy and tired that I did not even take the opportunity to look. The crossing of the Seine did not actually take place at Louviers because better crossing spots had been identified at points eastward toward Paris. When we finally found the right spot, our crossing was unopposed, and we landed on the east side of the Seine River, ready to proceed with our chase of the Germans through the rest of France toward Belgium and eventually Holland and Germany.

The start of the next phase of this chase to Germany will be the subject of the next Chapter.

Chapter 5

FROM PARIS TO THE SIEGFRIED LINE
August 1944 - December 1944

Map 5A
From Paris to the Siegfried Line

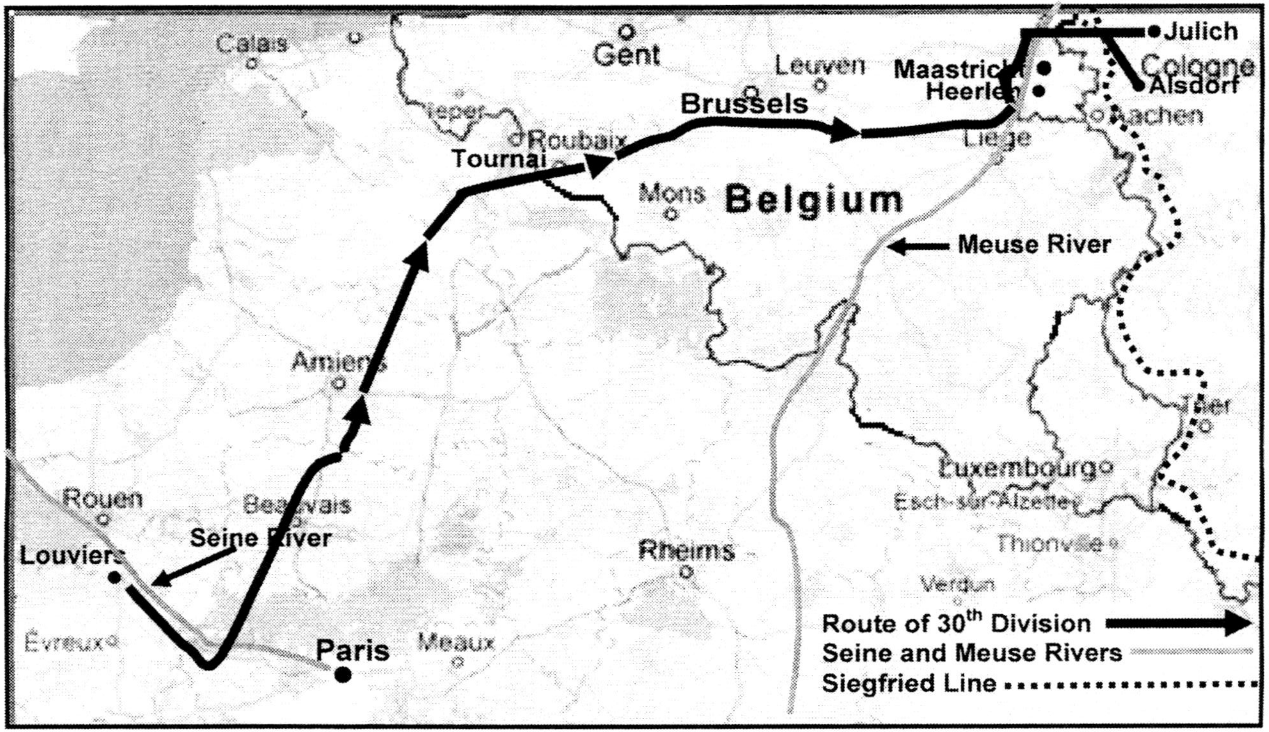

Map 5B Close-Up of Siegfried Line Area

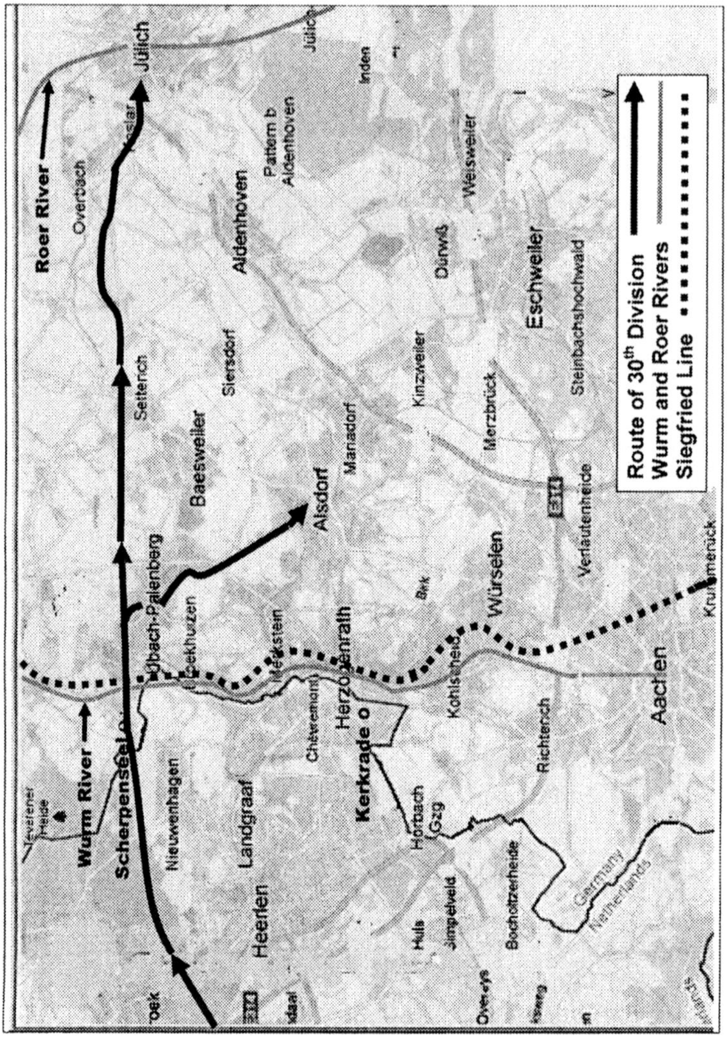

Chapter 5

FROM PARIS TO THE SIEGFRIED LINE
August 1944 - December 1944

When the German counterattack was stopped both at Saint Lo and Mortain, we were told that the Germans had made the decision to abandon their defense efforts in Normandy and retreat back toward Germany. It appears that their original retreat strategy included making a major defense stand along the Seine River. However, after losing major parts of its troops, supplies and equipment in the Falaise pocket, the German High Command apparently realized that their remaining forces were inadequate to make the Seine River stand, and their strategy shifted to making the next major stand along the Siegfried Line (known to the Germans as their West Wall).

This made it relatively easy for the Allied Forces to occupy Paris and then to cross the Seine River and start a pursuit of the Germans eastward and northward toward the German border. Our 30th Division was given the job of pursuing them northward through the northern part of France, through Belgium and the Netherlands, eventually to arrive at the Siegfried Line in the vicinity of Maastricht, Holland.

When Paris was occupied by the Allied Forces on August 25th, our 117th Regiment was waiting on the west bank of the Seine, near the town of Louviers. On August 27th, we were given the order to cross the Seine and proceed with our drive to the north and east. We did not cross the river exactly at Louviers, but rather moved along the west bank in the direction of Paris until we could find the most appropriate place to cross. As it turned out, we found such a spot where the Seine River made a northward and then a southward loop. On the inner side of the tip of this loop, I remember that there was a huge cement manufacturing plant, and we used the facilities that were provided there for making a mass crossing of the River. The crossing was made efficiently and quickly and with no enemy opposition.

Then began the long, fast drive to the north and then to the east, finally arriving at the Siegfried line in the vicinity of

Maastricht. It was about 400 miles and took us less than a month. I have heard it called the fastest opposed march in the history of warfare. To track our progress along this march, the reader is invited to refer to Map 5A, which is included at the beginning of this Chapter.

Although the pace was very fast, there were times of delay, primarily caused by running out of gas. We eventually found out that the interruption in our gas supply was caused by the difficulty our supply units had in keeping up with the speed of our advance. In the beginning our supplies of food, vehicles, gas, ammunition, and reinforcements were reaching us from the United States through the ports we had captured on the western coast of France. However, as we proceeded through Normandy and then northward and eastward toward Germany, the supply lines between us and the French western coast ports became overextended, and it was necessary to switch to ports that we had captured along the English Channel, such as the Normandy Beaches and Antwerp. Although these ports were closer, they had their disadvantages. The Normandy beaches had no docks for large ocean-going vessels, and, although we had liberated Antwerp, the U.S. supply ships who were trying to land there were constantly under German attack from the air. Once unloaded from the U.S. ships, the supplies had to be trucked from the ports to our inland positions. This was done by the famous Allied "Red Ball Express," whose trucks ran continuously for 20 hours each day. In spite of the great effort made by the Allied supply forces, there were times when we just outran them.

In our headlong race across France, Belgium and Holland, we received very warm welcome from the people who were being liberated. As we pulled into towns along the way, there would be thousands of people cheering us on and wanting us to stop and visit with them and have meals with them. At one place, even though we arrived after midnight, and it was very cold, the crowds were still out celebrating, and they had a big bonfire going, into which they had thrown anything and everything that reminded them of the Germans. There was cheering and laughing, and they were offering us wine and coffee and sandwiches and wanting us to stay. That would have

Ch. 5 - From Paris to the Siegfried Line

been nice, but our pace was too fast to allow it. When you pull into a town, sitting on the spare tire of a jeep behind a 50 caliber gun, there are other concerns, such as wondering if some hidden German sniper has you in his crosshairs, or, even, where is the bathroom?

During the entire period of bulldogging our way across France, Belgium and Holland, my Recon patrol group continued our mode of operation as previously described. Each morning we would drive our jeeps, equipped with scopes, radio and machine guns, to a point 23 miles ahead of our regimental battle, and send as much information back to headquarters about any retreating enemy troops as we could find. It was a month of severe pressure on the endurance of our regimental battle line, because they usually had to walk all the miles that were covered, and this went on day after day for the whole month.

On September 3rd, we crossed into Belgium and kept heading north in the general direction of Brussels. The pace at this point continued to be very rapid. Generally, we could go for long distances without any signs of resistance from the German Army, but then we would run into pockets where the Germans had decided to make a stand. At these points, the going became dangerous, not only for our Recon patrol operating both inside and outside of the enemy lines, but also for our 117th Regimental foot soldiers who were following behind. A taste of what was involved in these situations can be gained by reading the following release from the War Department that was received by my parents back home:

> "The quick thinking and sure-shooting of an alert three-some saved the 117th Infantry's I and R platoon from an ugly situation during a daring patrol inside enemy territory in Belgium recently. Private Daniel D. Smith, Seargent Scrage and Private Gaskill were the rear guard of a 15-man patrol in German lines on the lookout for information and prisoners. While the patrol was working its way along, Pvt. Gaskill saw 15 Germans in a position to bush-whack the 117th infantrymen. As he gave the warning, Pvt. Smith shot

and killed three of the enemy. Sgt. Scrage killed another, and the others were captured to take back for information purposes."

As we progressed northward in Belgium we reached and liberated the town of Tournai, Belgium. At this point we turned eastward and headed for Maastricht. This path took us through the outskirts of Brussels, Belgium, and an experience at this point stands out in my memory because this is where my jeep was stopped by Belgian police and we were notified that the Queen of Belgium, who lives in the Brussels vicinity, wanted us to come and visit her. My driver and I did in fact go with the police, and were greeted by the Queen and asked if we would stay overnight in her palace. We had to say "no" because our Regiment was on the move, but we did enjoy the highly rationed pad of butter and the cube of sugar that she gave us – an honor apparently bestowed only upon a favored few.

On September 10th, we crossed the Meuse River at the town of Liege and then turned north and followed the River up to Maastricht, which we then liberated. From there we moved a short distance to the east, to get to the Dutch town of Heerlen, and then finally, on September 19th, we moved another short distance and stopped in the German town of Scherpenseel.

The move to Scherpenseel involved crossing the German border, and, although the real barrier (the Siegfried Line) was still another mile away across beet fields and across the Wurm River to the east, we were now in German territory. Things all of a sudden were different. There were no civilians, and no friendly Dutch faces, only German soldiers sniping at us at every turn. Our progress slowed to a crawl, as we paused to bust down doors in farm houses, looking for snipers, and then finally arriving at Scherpenseel.

At Scherpenseel, we were confronted with the famous Siegfried Line. It was known to Germans as their Westwall. It was a system of defensive positions, stretching for long distances north and south along the western border of Germany. It did not rely on large fortifications but used terrain features and many belts of mutually supporting bunkers, pillboxes, and firing positions. These defenses, combined with minefields and antitank barriers such as "dragons' teeth" and deep ditches, protected the German border region. The forward defenses were backed by hardened bunkers for troops, supplies and command-and-control facilities. The operational concept was to slow attacking forces and create opportunities for counterattacks by mobile forces.

To track the events that are described in the remaining part of this Chapter, the reader is invited to refer to Map 5B, which is an enlargement of the Siegfried Line area extending from Scherpenseel down to Aachen.

The Allied strategy at this point was to have our 117th Regiment concentrate on breaking through the Siegfried Line in the Scherpenseel area, while other elements of the 30th Division would concentrate on breaking through at various points to the south of us. This included capturing the city of Aachen, which was also in Germany, but with the Siegfried line running from north to south in the Aachen eastern suburbs. The battle to capture Aachen was anticipated to be a very fiercely fought contest, because Aachen was a city that had a rich history and was dear in the hearts and emotions of most Germans and their leaders. It was a city that they would strenuously defend, and at all costs.

After a couple of days rest in Scherpenseel, while we waited for additional supplies and artillery and replacement troops to catch up with us, the order was given to start the attack against the Siegfried Line. To begin this, six of us in our Recon patrol got some sleep toward the end of the day and then, at nightfall, we took our scopes and crawled the mile through beet fields to the little village of Marienberg, which was located on the west bank of the Wurm River, just across from the Siegfried Line which was located on the east bank of the river. The Wurm River was actually a small, narrow stream, but with high banks and very muddy approaches.

We knew that Marienberg had been evacuated. There were no civilians around, only some military sentries at different points in the village. We encountered no land mines, and we circled the sentries and set up in the second story of an abandoned house, located just across the Wurm River from the Siegfried bunkers.

We had with us the two Karl Zeiss scopes, No. 2 and No. 12, that we had "acquired" on our way through France. They were heavy, but we dragged them with us when we crawled through the beet fields to reach Marienberg. From our second-story vantage point, they provided us with an excellent view of all the details of the Siegfried Line. We were all set up with everything we needed for updating the French maps that we had, and getting ready for sending firing directions to our artillery battalions behind us. We still needed a wire line to communicate with the artillery, and the wire section Master Sergeant himself crawled through the beet fields to bring us a telephone and wire.

The next day we started directing artillery fire against the bunkers and pill boxes of the Siegfried Line. In one of the many books that have been written about this attack, the author quoted me as follows:

> Daniel Smith, 117th I & R Platoon, said that his patrol activity intensified as time for the attack grew near. Two German Carl Zeiss scopes that had been picked up in France, one with 4" lenses weighing 50 pounds without the tripod (which weighed 40 pounds more), proved very useful. The two eyepieces rotated to give 12, 20 or 40 power. He recalled that they crawled and dragged that scope a mile at night through beet fields to a position from which to observe bunkers [across the river from Marienberg as well as the bunkers a half mile away in Ubach.] Then, on the next night, after the wire section master sergeant had given them a telephone and a reel of wire, he said "We were in business. With the help of the scope and oblique aerial photos, we updated the French maps by adding omitted pillboxes. We called fire on every fortification we saw, trying every weapon available, but with little effect. The conclusion was that only rifles, flamethrowers and torpedoes would work." That OP operated within German lines for five days.

Smith mentioned that when he got back, he was finally promoted to Pfc. He said that the first thing done daily on the OP was to knock off any enemy A.T. weapons and Ops that had been set up or replaced overnight.

>Charles B. McDonald,
>*The Siegfried Line Campaign,*
>Center of Military History - US Army
>Washington, D.C. 1963

As mentioned in the history book quoted above, during the five days we were in the Marienberg house, we called fire on the bunkers with every kind of shell that was available in our artillery and with all the 400 guns that we had, including three French coastal guns (6-inch, high velocity, mounted on open tank chassis). During this time, we received no counter battery, except when we fired the French coastal guns. These brought enough attention that there was counterfire from the German batteries, and two of our French guns were knocked out.

As it turned out in the end, all our artillery fire, even though it was the best we could muster, was to no avail. The damage to the Siegfried line bunkers and pillboxes was minimal. I informed Headquarters that the only thing that would work would be to have our men get up close and fire rifles, flame throwers and grenades through the slits.

After five days, we returned to Headquarters in Sherpenseel. Everybody was surprised to see that we had survived. I was promoted to Pfc., and this is where I was awarded the Silver Star.

We learned that other elements of the 30th Division had similarly been turned back in their efforts against the Siegfried Line at various points to the south of us between us and Aachen.. We also learned that the Allied High Command had determined that our allied forces were not yet ready to make this kind of attack on the Siegfried Line, and the operation was being put on hold in order to get more time to bring up more troops, supplies, artillery and ammunition. The delay would also give us time to develop a different kind of strategy for this kind of situation and to train our troops in the new kind of approach.

In the new strategy, the attack was to be preceded by a saturation bombing from the air, to disrupt enemy communications and disorganize the enemy firing positions. The aerial bombing was to be accompanied by artillery fire from our 400 available artillery guns. The main thrust was to be carried out by infantry troops moving on foot to reach the Wurm River, to cross it on specially made bridges, and to surround and capture each pillbox or bunker by use of rifles, bazookas, flame throwers and grenades.

The delay that was imposed was for a period of about ten days. During that time, the 30th Division underwent intensive crosstraining to renew skills that had been lost through attrition of personnel in the preceding months of combat. All assault battalions relearned skills in rapid river crossing and in assaulting and reducing fortified positions. The line companies were retrained in the use of rifles, bazookas and the other weapons that would be used. The Engineering battalions built improvised bridging, using a replica of the Wurm River with its steep banks. The replica was made from a ditch of stagnant water for crossing and bridging practice.

At Headquarters, an accurate 12 x 5 foot sand table was constructed, using the maps and information that we had accumulated on the earlier attack. In the training sessions, each of the line regiments was assigned specific numbers of specific pillboxes or bunkers to be knocked out. The sand table was very useful in the training sessions to identify the specific targets that each regimental unit was responsible for.

During the delay, there was also time for rest and relaxation. I got a two-day pass down to the town of Kerkrade

Then, on October 2, the full-scale attack began. In our particular segment of the war, this involved attacks by the various regiments of the 30th Division against the Siegfried line in multiple locations extending from our northerly position at Scherpenseel down to the City of Aachen. Our 117th Regiment was responsible for the attack in the Scherpenseel area.

Ch. 5 - From Paris to the Siegfried Line

The preliminary aerial attack proved to be ineffective. As in the case of Saint Lo, the medium bombers approached from the wrong angle and were off target. Fortunately, only a few bombs fell where they hurt our men. On the other hand, except for that initial disappointment, our attack operation starting at Scherpenseel was a complete success. Our line troops trotted the distance between Scherpenseel and the Wurm River, and arrived there exactly synchronized in time with the Engineering Battalion, who threw their temporary bridges across the Wurm and allowed the line regiments to cross and move in on their assigned pillboxes and bunkers.

The bunkers were spaced about 100 yards apart, and three teams of American foot soldiers worked together with rifles to take each bunker – one team against the center and one team against each side. There was intensive opposition, but our regimental numbers overwhelmed the defending Germans, and the breakthrough was accomplished by the end of the day. Later information told us that 39 pillboxes had been knocked out, to provide the opening which allowed columns of our troops to move through the Siegfried line into German territory east of the Line.

Two of our regimental companies abreast came through the opening for a mile the first day. Then they turned right at Ubach for 5,000 yards the second day to run south behind the eastern side of the pillboxes and bunkers. The agreement was that if we got through, the 2nd Armored would pass through us. I liked the 2nd Armored. They welded their ammunition boxes to the tanks and fillled them with concrete. They were good. They went through Ubach all buttoned up, This is where I got hit by a brick from a part of a church steeple. The 2nd Armored went southward to assist the elements of our Army that were involved in breaking through the Siegfried Line at places like Kerkrade, and especially to join the fight to capture Aachen.

We ourselves took a slightly different path southward and ended up in Alsdorf where we set up in an artillery observation post on the fourth floor of an apartment in the front lines. From this post we could see all traffic going in and out of Aachen. It was surrounded on three sides by the 1st Division. Each morning we would identify and put out of business their artillery observers and antitank guns, and then harass the road into Aachen. This lasted for about two weeks. With our glasses, there was no way for them to hide an artillery observer.

One morning I went to the observation post alone. As I got there, a barrage of huge artillery shells hit the building. I made a dive for the basement. I thought the building would sink. When the Germans stopped firing, after 8 or 9 rounds, I found a dud. It had passed through a brick wall, and through a concrete floor and had lodged in the chimney of the kitchen. It was very hot and was about 11 inches in diameter and about three feet long. It had come from a railroad gun. My valuable Carl Zeiss scope lay under a pile of brick. One of the eye pieces was knocked off. The front wall of the building was gone, and our firing data that was written on the wallpaper was also gone.

The next day, however (October 16th), word came that the Germans had given up the battle and had evacuated Aachen. The big railroad gun barrage that they had fired against us was the last thing they had done before pulling out of Aachen and retreating eastward toward the Roer River. I think the reason they sent that huge barrage against our Alsdorf location was to put us out of commission so that our artillery would not fire on them on the roads leading out of Aachen as they started their retreat.

The breaking of the Siegfried Line had been accomplished. The city of Aachen had been captured. Our Regiment set up its Headquarters in Alsdorf, and we were allowed time to get some rest and recreation and to start the preparations for the next phase of our eastward drive – namely, the crossing of the Roer River.

The strategy for the next phase was to move eastward into position just west of the town of Julich, which is located on the Roer River (not to be confused with the Ruhr River). The Roer River had become the next major defense stand of the German military. It was known that our crossing of the Roer would be hotly contested, and dangerous, because the Germans had control of a number of Roer River upstream dams, which they could blow up and cause

Ch. 5 - From Paris to the Siegfried Line

uncontrollable flooding in the areas where we would want to cross. The Allied High Command did not want to attempt the crossing until we had time to increase our supplies of ammunition, gas, artillery, etc. and to build up the numbers of personnel in our regimental forces.

Therefore, after Aachen fell and when we got our brief period of rest, we were ordered to go back to the Heerlen/Scherpenseel area and then proceed eastward to Julich and then stop, awaiting further orders before attempting to cross the Roer. We did in fact move over to Julich. The Siegfried Line had been broken, so it was not difficult to get through the line. The rest of the way eastward toward Julich was contested all the way, but the German resistance was scattered and disorganized because the Germans were intent on building up their resources to make a stand at the Roer. We were able to arrive in the area of Julich without suffering any major losses.

We did not attempt to cross the Roer River at this time. Instead, we returned to our Regimental Headquarters in Alsdorf and waited for the Allied High Command to give the order to go back to Julich and cross the Roer. We knew there would be a fairly long period of wait, and we were given an additional opportunity for rest and relaxation, including passes to nearby places of interest in the area, such as casinos where we watched dancing girls and heard Marlene Dietrich sing, and other places where we could sleep in real beds

Then, in the middle of all this came the news that the Germans were launching a last ditch counteroffensive drive from Germany westward through the Ardennes area south of us. This was an attempt to drive all the way to the west coast of Belgium and isolate the Allied forces north of their drive line and thus hopefully bring the Allied forces to their knees and at least create a situation where Germany could negotiate a more favorable peace settlement. This German drive became known as the Battle of the Bulge (also known as the Ardennes Offensive).

We were in Alsdorf at the time, and were given orders to go to Heerlen and organize our regiments and then proceed immediately to the south to add our strength to the opposition against this counterattack.

The story of our participation in the Battle of the Bulge will be the subject of the next chapter.

Ch. 5 - From Paris to the Siegfried Line

Chapter 5 Pictures from Dan Smith's Album

Fig. 10 - Recon Unit Scouting Belgian Countryside in Front of Advancing 117th Regiment

Fig. 11 - Another 117th Recon Unit in the Drive Across Belgium

Fig. 12. - Dan Smith With Kids in Belgian Village

Fig. 13 - Dan Smith in Germany, Waiting for Orders to Crash the Siegfried Line

Fig. 14 - Dan Smith Being Awarded the Silver Star for Bravery in Reaching and Maintaining a Forward Observation Post Under Heavy Enemy Concentrations of Artillery Fire, and Providing Crucial Information that Enabled Piercing of the Siegfried Line.

Chapter 6

THE BATTLE OF THE BULGE
December 1944 - January 1945

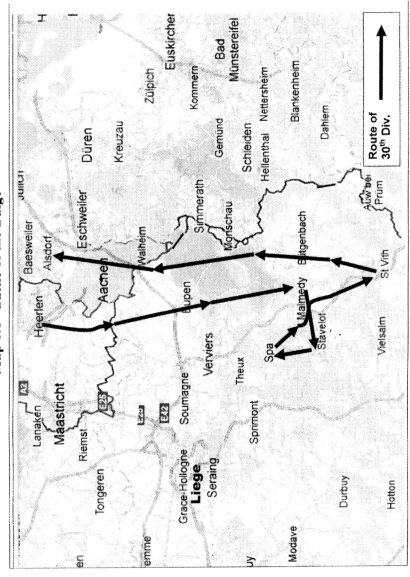

Map 6A - Battle of the Bulge

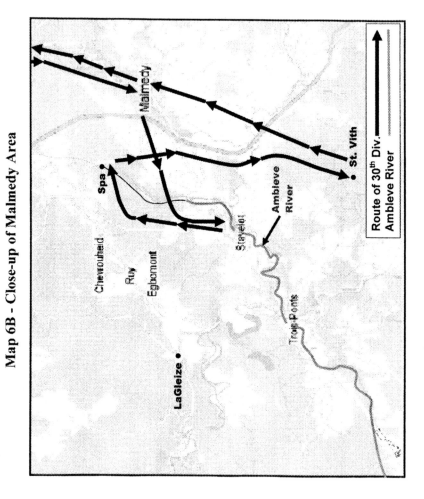

Map 6B - Close-up of Malmedy Area

Chapter 6

THE BATTLE OF THE BULGE
December 1944 - January 1945

After breaking through the Siegfried Line and capturing Aachen, we were waiting in our regimental headquarters at Alsdorf, Germany, for the signal to proceed with the difficult crossing of the Roer River. The buildup of personnel, supplies, equipment, artillery, etc., that was needed for this was taking a fair amount of time. This gave us some leisure time, and we were going over to places like Heerlen and Maastrich and other places where we could find entertainment and relaxation – and even a place to take a shower.

After a whole month of battling our way through France, Belgium and Holland, sleeping on the ground all the way, listening to planes and shells all night long, and never having a shower, our passes to Heerlen offered another unexpected benefit. Heerlen was a coal mining town, and coal mines provide shower facilities. We indulged ourselves in taking showers. On one visit to Heerlen we were at a mine that had two trailers with shower equipment. Since there were a lot of us from the Regiment, the ritual was that we would take off all our clothes and pass through the shower rooms in a steady line. As we moved through, we were allowed one minute for a wet-down, two minutes to soap, and two minutes to rinse, and then out. On this particular visit, when we were in the middle of all this, an ME109 came zooming in on us, and a lot of naked soldiers went scattering for shelter. It must have been funny because everybody was laughing. At any rate, I stayed behind and had a glorious 10 minutes of showering all to myself.

Then, when we were on another visit to Heerlen, I remember that we were in an ice cream parlor at about 1:00 in the afternoon, and we were suddenly ordered back to our units. Apparently an unexpected crisis had arisen because the Germans had launched a surprise counterattack in the Ardenne region that lay about 50 miles to the south of us. Although we did not know what to call it at the time, the counterattack later came to be known as the Battle of the Bulge. Our regiment and the rest of the Division were ordered to assemble in Heerlen. This was accomplished by 7:00 p.m. of the same day, and we immediately started the march southward.

We were to march all night long, with the objective of reaching the Belgian town of Malmedy in the morning. For this headlong drive, my platoon led the way, followed by our 117th Regiment and the rest of the 30th Division, followed by the Regiment's tanks. Our platoon had six jeeps. I was in the lead jeep with its mounted 50 caliber machine gun. As we passed through small towns, we would drop off jeeps one at a time to guide the blind tanks through the town square and road junctions. I don't remember the names of the roads we took or the towns we passed through. I do know that we did not pass through Aachen, but rather took a road down through Belgium that passed slightly west of Aachen.

At this point in the story I should pause to describe a couple of different facets of this Battle of the Bulge experience for the reader to keep in mind throughout this entire chapter. In the first place, it should be remembered that the entire experience took place in December and January, in the dead of the winter. Most of the time we were traveling on hard, frozen, icy, slippery, or muddy ground. There were even times when I lost the use of my jeep and had to walk from one place to another. Sometimes, the most important battle was to protect against frostbite on hands and feet, and, at all odds, to keep from freezing to death.

In the second place, it should be kept in mind that the Ardennes area that we were going into was a place of utmost confusion. Both the Allied forces and the German forces were confused. It was hard to know where the battle lines were drawn. Prior to the start of the German Bulge counterattack, the Allied forces' front line had pushed all the way east to the Roer River, and everything west of that front line was held by the Allies. However, early in December, the Germans had secretly gathered all the forces they could muster and had started a counterattack back toward the west. They had broken through the Allied front line position at the Roer River in the Ardennes and other areas and had pushed for many miles westward, recapturing many towns and taking Allied prisoners. Their objective was to drive toward and recapture Leige, Belgium, and then, ultimately to continue on to recapture Antwerp on the west coast of Belgium, and thus trap all the Allied forces which were north of the line of their drive.

The point to keep in mind, therefore, is that we were about to arrive in the Malmedy area, which was right in the middle of the front edge of the Germans' westward counterattack, and, as mentioned, this area was in utter confusion. If we turned in one direction, we would run into a German battalion, but if we turned in another we would be joining an Allied battalion. Some Allied forces had become so confused that they actually surrendered to the Germans. In one German battalion that was captured and taken prisoner, the German soldiers spoke English and had American uniforms under their German uniforms. This was the status of the area into which our all-night drive from Heerlen was to enter.

Getting back to our story, as our platoon led the all-night drive toward Malmedy, German planes were constantly dropping flares ahead of us, checking on us. We learned to ignore them. Then, when we were in a small town near the end of our trip, a large red flare was dropped to the south of us, behind some buildings, and continued to burn on the ground, lighting up the overcast sky blood red. At the same time, a large German tri-motor transport plane approached from the east, flying very low and slow, as if in a landing pattern. I immediately engaged the plane and put a whole box of one hundred shells into the plane. I never saw the plane crash, but a couple of weeks later I learned that it had indeed crashed, and that a German commander and two paratroopers had jumped just before the crash and had been captured. The remaining paratroopers in the plane had perished.

The story behind the paratrooper episode is that, at Hitler's orders, a German paratrooper school had been set up in German territory near the Roer River. The plan was that, when ready, a fleet of German transport planes would carry 1,000 paratroopers to a point west of the Allied forces who were defending against the German counterattack, and then the Allied forces would be sandwiched between the westward-moving main German counterattack and the 1,000 paratroopers who would have landed to the west of them. When the fleet of over 100 transport planes took off, the Commander of the paratrooper school was in the lead plane, and this is the plane that I shot down. When the rest of the German fleet saw what had happened, they turned around and went back to Germany. The 1,000 paratroopers in those planes were ordered then to get out of the planes and march on the ground back to the west to join the battles. They never made it.

Several years after World War II, I read a book that had been written by Friedrich von der Heydte, the German paratroop school commander who had been in the lead transport plane and had been shot down and captured. In his book, Von der Heydte described the experience as follows:

> "I jumped with a broken arm, two sergeants jumped with me, both broke bones. The 124 planes returned to Germany, they tried to get involved, but roads were so poor and crowded that they never were a factor."

I often wonder what would have happened if I had not shot down the lead plane. The Battle of the Bulge was fiercely contested, with opposing forces of almost equal strength, and the outcome was narrowly in balance until the very end, when the Allied forces finally prevailed. If those 124 German transport planes had continued on their mission and successfully dropped their 1,000 paratroopers behind Allied lines, who knows if this might have been enough to tip the balance in favor of the Germans and allowed them to drive on to recapture Liege and then Antwerp.

At any rate, getting back to the story of our all-night drive toward Malmedy, with the paratrooper incident behind us, it was getting to be daylight, and, as we approached Malmedy, we could see battalions of German tanks lined up in the hills to the east of us. It looked as if they were poised to move out at any moment, either against us, or against Malmedy, or on to some other destination

Ch. 6 - The Battle of the Bulge

unknown to us. We did not attempt to engage them, but continued on into Malmedy, arriving early in the morning.

When we arrived, Malmedy was in a shambles and in disarray. The Germans thought they had captured the town, but there were active allied forces still in the town, contesting the recapture. The first thing we heard when we got there was that one area of the town was being used by the Germans as a prison camp where the Germans were collecting surrendered Allied soldiers and that, a short time earlier, a German SS Panzer unit had marched about 150 American prisoners to a field and massacred them – obviously a grave violation of the Geneva Convention. I heard later that Joachim Peiper, the commander of the SS unit and SS General Josef Dietrich, who ordered the shooting of the American prisoners of war, were put on trial during the Dachau Trials in 1946. Peiper was sentenced to death, but his sentence was later commuted to life imprisonment. Dietrich was sentenced to 25 years in prison. However, both of them were released from prison about 10 years later.

We were not in Malmedy very long when we were ordered to proceed down to Stavelot to join the battle that was raging for control of that town. Our reconnaissance patrol was split into two parts, and I was given control of one of these parts, with orders to lead units of the 17th Regiment troops and artillery over to the area where we could support the allied defense of Stavelot.

Stavelot needed defensive help, because Columns of troops and tanks in Josef Dietrich's SS Panzer Army (some of whom apparently had participated in the Malmedy massacre) had continued southward and westward down to attempt to capture Stavelot, which is a key town on the main highway to Liege. Stavelot was a small town (population 5,000) that lay in the Ambleve River valley, surrounded by high wooded bluffs. Most of the town was built on the north bank of the river or on the slopes above. There were a few scattered buildings on the south bank. The Ambleve River north of Stavelot was a fairly shallow stream which was no particular obstacle to infantry, vehicles and tanks wishing to cross it. However, at Stavelot the valley of the river was deeply enclosed by high cliffs on both sides, such that troops and tanks were unable to cross without the presence of a bridge; and, as a matter of fact there was one, and only one, vehicular bridge at Stavelot. The only approach to this bridge from the east was by the main highway, and at this point the ground to the left of the highway fell away sharply, and the ground to the right sloped steeply above the highway.

Farther south on the Amblevé River was the town of Trois Ponts. This town was at a crossroad of roads, and it was at this point that the Amblevé joined one of its tributaries, the Salm River. Trois Ponts gained its name because it had three vehicular bridges, two over the Salm and one over the Amblevé.

General Dietrich's intelligence sources told him that the town of Stavelot was heavily populated with Allied troops and guns, and, in order to build up more of his Panzer units and supplies, he hesitated for a time before attempting to cross the one bridge into Stavelot. After some delay, he finally sent an initial number of troops and tanks across the bridge, and what followed was some very intensive street fighting in the neighborhoods of Stavelot. General Dietrich was dissatisfied with the progress of his attempt to get through Stavelot and, at one point, used some of the troops and tanks still waiting to cross the bridge to attempt an end run to the southwest through Trois Ponts and then back up to the town of LaGleize, which is on the main highway to Leige. However, because of the almost impassable roads that were encountered on the way to Trois Ponts, this effort failed.

It was at this point that my patrol unit and its following troops and artillery arrived at the scene. We wanted to get to the hills north and east of Stavelot, where we could look down on Stavelot and the surrounding countryside. We did this by proceeding from Malmedy westward so that we could cross the Amblevé several miles north of Stavelot, where the river was shallow and crossable, and then we were able to come in from behind and climb up the hill on the northeast edge of Stavelot. From this vantage point, with our scopes, we were able to see all of Stavelot and the Panzer troops and tanks which had not yet crossed the bridge, and we could even see Trois Ponts to the west and LaGleize to the northwest.

When we got there we discovered that the Allied engineers had finally succeeded in dynamiting the Stavelot bridge across the Ambleve River. The scores of Panzer tanks which had not yet crossed the bridge were trapped in the narrow highway that approached the bridge. For two days, our patrol unit directed artillery fire with great intensity into this column of trapped tanks. The tanks and supporting vehicles were destroyed. The tank crews and supporting troops left their tanks and vehicles and tried to retreat back toward the east but were instantly surrounded and captured by advancing Allied forces.

Without the Ambleve bridge, Dietrich's Panzer troops that had already crossed into Stavelot were isolated. Their fuel and other supplies coming from the east were completely cut off, and Dietrich's effort to conquer and pass through Stavelot withered and died. The freeway to Leige and the Meuse River which Dietrich's Panzers were supposed to open for the following divisions of the Panzer Army remained nothing more than a dead end. By December 20, Dietrich's Panzer troops had abandoned the attempt to drive through Stavelot.

While we were in our position high on the hill on the northeast side of Stavelot, we witnessed, but did not participate in, another critical battle that had been going on concurrently with Dietrich's Panzer efforts at Stavelot. This was an effort by other elements of the German Army to bring battalions of tanks from their position in the hills east of Malmedy on an end-run drive westward across the Ambleve north of Stavelot and then over to LaGleize, which is north of Stavelot and on the main highway to Leige. (These apparently were the battalions of German tanks which we saw in the eastern hills on the morning when we were arriving from the north on our all-night drive into Malmedy.) These German tank battalions did in fact arrive in LaGlieze and were preparing to continue on to Leige, but they were attacked and destroyed by American Air Force bombers. We watched it all from our vantage point above Stavelot.

As an interesting side note to the LaGleize incident, I later read that a Belgian reporter and photographer had actually joined the German tanks east of Malmedy and had ridden with them, recording everything, while they drove westward north of Stavelot and around to LaGleize. He watched and photographed and recorded as the tanks were being destroyed, and then, after the war, he stayed in LaGleize and played a part in collecting tank parts and weapons and other memorabilia from the battle, for building a museum on the spot where it all happened. The museum still exists today.

With the German Panzer drive through Stavelot and LaGleize successfully brought to a solid end by December 20th, our scout patrol and accompanying artillery units were ordered to move to Spa, Belgium, a small town a few miles north and west of Malmedy. Spa is where the 117th Regiment had set up its headquarters. Our patrol unit took up lodgings in a large barn on a farm on the outskirts of Spa. From this point, we would eat our meals at Regimental Headquarters in Spa, and from here we were ordered at various times to go out and reinforce Allied defense efforts at hotly contested battles, such as Almedy, St. Vith, etc.

At one point our Regiment went down to Almedy and participated in the skirmishes for about a week. I remember that the snow was very, very deep, and that the battle had slowed considerably. Then, however, in the middle of this slowdown, Almedy became the target of opportunity for American B-26 bombers. They bombed the town, apparently unaware that, in addition to the Germans, there were U.S. troops as well as civilians in the town. It was Saint Lo all over again. They came back twice more and destroyed what was left of Almedy. We lost some good G.I.s in those attacks, as well as over 100 civilians who were killed.

One note of interest that I remember about Almedy is that the American General Hospital that was located there was evacuated, but in the departure they left so fast that a lot of good whiskey was left behind. I remember putting this whiskey in five gallon water cans and giving one of them to each of our companies. In the intense cold, I took care of the guys in our scouting patrols by cutting up spare blankets to make vests, shoe liners, and liners for everybody's sleeping bags. We simply could not operate in the cold galoshes we were issued.

At another time, we were sent to St. Vith, which was a few miles south and east of Malmedy, and where there was intensive fighting going on. The venture still sticks in my mind because the weather was so cold and icy and miserable, that I could not even use my jeep to get there but had to walk all the way. At the end of our stay there, St. Vith had become obliterated like Malmedy.

By this time, in this part of the Battle of the Bulge theater, the German counterattack efforts were petering out, and the Germans were starting to make their retreat back toward the original battle lines that had been drawn at the Roer River. Generally speaking, the German Ardennes counterattack had consisted of three major prongs, known as the north, middle and south prongs, all headed westward toward the Belgian west coast. The efforts of our Regiment had been in the north prong, and on this prong the German drive had been completely repulsed. The same was true in the south prong. However, Allied forces defending the middle prong were intensely besieged, especially at the key road junction of Bastogne. On December 22nd the Allied forces in Bastogne appeared to be in a hopeless position, but nevertheless held on. Then, the clearing of the weather on December 24th allowed the Allied Air Force to drop supplies and attack the enemy lines, and Allied reinforcement troops arrived. By December 26th, the German advance came to an end and Bastogne was saved. I did not take part in the defense of Bastogne, but I tip my hat to the brave soldiers who did.

That was the end of the Battle of the Bulge. The US First and Third Armies launched a counteroffensive and this continued until January 28th, 1945, when the Germans were finally pushed back to the line which existed before December 16th when the Battle of the Bulge began.

The failed German Ardennes Offensive was not only a blow to German morale, but it caused significant depletion of the German Army. German casualties were estimated to be in excess of 100,000 Germans killed, wounded or captured. Moreover, many of the German troops that were lost had been borrowed from the manpower being used to defend against the westward movement of the Russian Army coming from the east toward Berlin, and this weakening of the defense allowed the Russian Army to pick up momentum in its attacks. The Battle of the Bulge was a major Allied victory and virtually destroyed any hopes for a German victory in the war. Nazi Germany was on its knees and the Allied victory in World War II became only a matter of time.

With the Battle of the Bulge interlude successfully behind us, we packed up and returned to Regimental Headquarters in Alsdorf, ready to get reorganized and take on the difficult crossing of the Roer River.

Ch. 6 - The Battle of the Bulge   79

Chapter 6 Pictures
from Dan Smith's Album

Fig. 15 - Scouting Operations in the Snowy Malmedy Area

Fig.. 16 - More Scouting Around Malmedy

Fig. 17 - Dan Smith in Position Above Stavelot

Fig. 18 - Dan in Position Above Stavelot

Ch. 6 - The Battle of the Bulge

Fig 19 - Dan in the Woods Above Stamelot

Fig. 20 - The Battle of the Bulge Was Fought in the Dead of Winter

Chapter 7

CROSSING THE ROER RIVER
February 1945

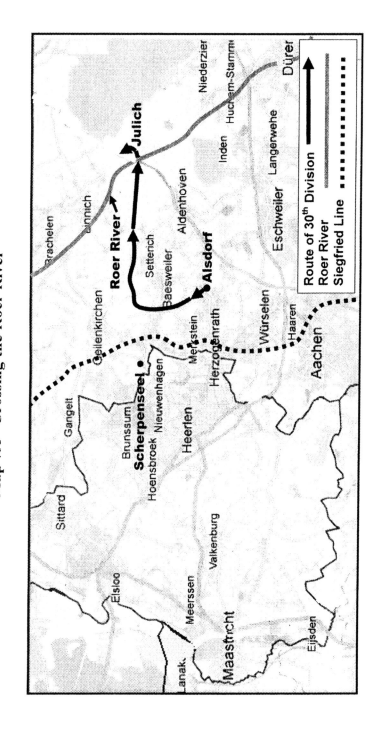

Map 7A - Crossing the Roer River

Chapter 7

CROSSING THE ROER RIVER
February 1945

Before being interrupted by the Battle of the Bulge, we had broken through the Siegfried Line and had captured Aachen and were in a waiting period, in the process of building up our resources and strategies for making an eastward drive across the Roer River at Julich.

After achieving a significant victory in the Battle of the Bulge, we traveled back north to our Regimental Headquarters in Altsdorf and resumed preparations for crossing the Roer. The Allied High Command's strategy at this point was not only to use the 30th Division to drive across the Roer in the vicinity of Julich, but also to use numerous other elements of the Allied Armies to cross the Roer at numerous other points, both north and south of Julich. This was to be a coordinated attack, with all the participating Allied Armies launching their crossings up and down the river at approximately the same time. This was regarded as an extremely difficult and critical phase of the War, and the Allied High Command was taking deliberately careful efforts to be fully and properly prepared.

When our 30th Division had left to spend two months fighting the Battle of the Bulge, other Divisions had been left behind in the Heerlen/Julich area to work on the preparations for the Roer River crossing. In addition the 75th Division was moved into the area to participate in the preparations. The 75th Division had been almost demolished in previous stages of the drive across Normandy, and was being rebuilt with green, hastily trained replacement troops. All of these were the forces we rejoined when we completed the Battle of the Bulge and moved back into the area.

Although all of our 117th Regiment Line and Artillery troops participated in these preparations, my reconnaissance patrol did not.

Our time was consumed in making preparations for setting up observation posts in the Julich area so that when the crossing date finally arrived, we would be in a position to do our usual thing — namely, send our Regimental Command all the necessary information on the terrain on both sides of the River, as well as the location of any enemy personnel or artillery placements, and then, at the proper time direct the artillery fire from our artillery units behind us.

As mentioned, the preparations and strategies for making the crossing were taking an exceptionally long time – much more than any previous river crossings. The downside of this was that it also allowed the enemy an equal amount of time to make their preparations for defense of the crossings that were anticipated up and down the length of the river.

Finally, in the early part of February, 1945, it appeared that we were ready to get the command to launch the crossing, but immediately our schedule suffered another setback because we received word that that Germans had released flood waters from the dams located in the upstream headwaters of the Roer River. The enemy apparently had enough information on our preparations to know when the launch of the crossing was to take place, and they timed the flood waters to arrive at our crossing points at the critical time of our crossings. Fortunately, the Allied High Command got word of the release of this water and immediately postponed the launch date. The flood waters at their peak made a violent current (as much as 7 miles per hour), through which no crossing could possibly succeed. Our Engineers had enough information to estimate when the upstream reservoirs would be emptied and when the flow of water would be sufficiently subsided at each of the Allied crossing points to make the crossings possible again. The Allied High Command strategy changed at this point to leave it to the various regimental commanders along the river to make their crossing at their first safe time.

All of this resulted in another delay of about ten days. It also created another serious obstacle to the crossing of the river. Although the flow of water eventually subsided, it left a much wider river, with dangerously muddied banks on both side of the river, where numerous Allied vehicles would become mired in the mud and out of commission. Besides this, it should be remembered that this was in February and the mud and water were icy cold.

We knew several days in advance that the first safe time for the crossing was going to be February 24th, and my reconnaissance patrol group went to our established observation point near Julich and started communications with the Headquarters and Artillery commands. The remarkable thing that we immediately noticed was that there was little if any information for us to report. There was no sign of any enemy troops and no sign of any artillery placements capable of firing on us when we made the crossing. It was hard for us to believe, but that is what we reported.

Although the estimated first safe date was February 24th, the 117th Regimental Command made a strategic decision to jump into the crossing a day early, even though the crest of the flood had not completely passed. The purpose was to catch the enemy by surprise. Therefore, the actual crossing started shortly after midnight on February 23rd. At the start of the crossing, our Artillery started a heavy wave of saturation bombing on the far side of the river, in order to disorganize and distract any enemy troops that might be under cover on that side. My reconnaissance group did not direct any of this bombing, because it did not involve any specific targets but rather was in the category of area bombing. Our reconnaissance group did not direct area bombing, only target bombing.

The actual crossing of the river was highly successful, and the entire 117th Regiment was able to reach the far shore and proceed to positions located several thousands of yards beyond the river by the end of the day on February 23rd. The Corps and Regimental Engineers had done a remarkable job of planning and providing for numerous ways for the troops, vehicles and supplies to cross the river. Troops were able to move across on footbridges and on barges, rafts, and other types of boats. Vehicles and tanks were able to make the crossing on treadway bridges that were quickly put in place. Troop-carrying Alligator tanks carried great numbers of personnel across. Supplies were transported on vehicles across the treadway bridges and were also ferried across on barges. The operation was an astounding success. The surprise again was that there was no opposition from the enemy.

Although the crossing was successful, this is not to say that there were no obstacles. In the first place, the stretch of land leading to the river was swampy and partially inundated, and a great amount of instantaneous roadwork had to be done to make the area passable for vehicles and troops. Besides this, the whole area was crossed with many barbed wire fences that had to be overrun. And then, on top of this, was the fact that the entire area was full of land mines, both on the west and east sides of the river. Locating and removing these mines was a dangerous but essential job. I remember seeing guys from the Engineering Corps, down on their hands and knees in the mud, digging out the mines with their hands and carrying them over to a disposal area.

Another obstacle was the heavy layer of smoke that we ourselves had laid down over the area on the far side of the river. As part of the defensive measures that we had taken at the time the crossing began, we had fired smoke-bearing artillery shells to protect us when we reached the other side of the river, but of course when our troops got there it not only protected us but also made it very difficult ourselves to see and to carry out our objectives.

My crossing of the river came later in the day when the operation had become calmer and everything was under control. Our Reconnaissance unit merely rode across on a barge. My jeep followed on a later barge. There was no enemy fire as we crossed. In fact, the only thing of this nature came when we got to the other side and were still on the muddy plain leading up to some buildings further away from the river, when we saw a German Stuka coming at us from downstream of the river. I had my binoculars under my shirt, and I could see him coming at us, ready to release his bombs. However, at this time in history, Stukas were practically obsolete, with very poor maneuverability, and we had no trouble avoiding the bombs that he sent at us. When we saw the bombs coming we just dodged right or left and got out of their way. However, outside of

Ch. 7 - Crossing the Roer River

this one incident, our 117th Regiment encountered absolutely no enemy resistance – a very surprising thing.

Since that time, I have often looked back and reflected on this. We knew, and this was confirmed in later years in all the accounts of the crossing of the Roer, that the crossings at most of the points upstream and downstream from where we crossed at Julich, were very intense and bloody battles, in which Allied units suffered heavy losses. Why were we so lucky? Speculating on the reason for this is a pretty complex exercise, but I think there are some facts that at least partially explain what happened.

In the first place, I think we have to give credit to the strategy planning that our Regimental command used in launching the crossing. We knew that the Germans were expecting an Allied unit to attempt the crossing at Julich, and Germans probably thought they had the defensive forces and strategies in place to stop such a crossing, because crossing right into the main section of the town of Julich had some serious disadvantages for the attacking Allied forces. At this point, the plain on the west side of the river was completely flat and devoid of buildings or other terrace features in which to hide. However, on the other side of the river, the town of Julich was high above the river with many, many buildings in which to hide troops and gun emplacements, and the Germans probably had such troops and gun emplacements in place.

Faced with this, our Regimental Command used two kinds of strategic surprise that apparently turned out to be effective. First, they did not launch the attack into the main part of Julich, but rather at a place that was a mile or so upstream, where there were obviously no buildings to hide in on either side of the river, and where there obviously were no enemy gun emplacements. Secondly, they launched the attack one day earlier than the Germans had expected.

Added to this is the fact that, when we assembled our 30th Division troops for the crossing in the Julich area, we took deliberate steps to conceal the fact that we were the 30th Division. We removed all Division patches from our uniforms and from our vehicles. We did this because we had intelligence reports that the

Germans were well aware of the power and effectiveness of the 30th Division. It was the 30th Division that shredded the German forces in the breakthrough of the Siegfried Line, and it was the 30th Division again that shredded the Germans in the Battle of the Bulge. It could very well have been that, when German reconnaissance units looked at the troops we were assembling, they concluded that they were looking at the green, poorly trained replacement troops of the 75th Division, and decided that they could afford to leave the Julich area unprotected, at least for a period of time, while they deployed their resources to other places along the river. At any rate, this misconception, together with the two surprise maneuvers (i.e., the attack at a different place and the unexpected earliness of the attack) apparently combined to catch the Germans off-guard, and unable to recover from their mistake, and we were able to make the complete crossing without any opposition.

Getting back to the account of my own crossing of the river, after the Stuka incident while we were on the plain just east of the river, we ran to a small building that we thought might serve as a temporary hiding place while we awaited orders for the next move. However, once we got inside the building we discovered that it was a German storage place for land mines. We decided that this was not a very good place to hide, so we moved further inland and found a two story farm building that had been vacated by the Germans. This is where we stayed for several days while we awaited orders for the next move – which was to be the crossing of the Rhine River.

Members of our own regimental command staff also moved into the building, and it became the Regimental Headquarters for a brief period of time. It turned out that this same building had been headquarters for a German regiment, and we found supplies of telephones, heaters, and other luxuries down in the basement. While we were there, I hooked up the telephones and the heaters so there was one in every room, and we enjoyed a more civilized life for the period of time we were there.

There was also a supply of radios in the basement, and I went up into the attic to see if I could string an aerial for the radios. When I got up there I discovered that the attic had been used by the farmer

Ch. 7 - Crossing the Roer River

to store or horde wheat. There was wheat everywhere up there, with hardly a place to walk. When I finally found what looked like some open flooring in the attic and started walking on it I discovered that it was only a thin sheet of insulation, and on my first step I came crashing down through this layer, sending debris all over some of the guys who were playing cards in the room below. They looked up, and all they could see was a pair of legs. I was wedged in. They had to come up and lift me out of where I was wedged. It must have been funny because they were laughing and having a lot of fun.

In the basement there was also a fleet of German motorcycles. I went down to look at them, along with my jeep driver who was from the hills of Tennessee. I got on one of the motorcycles and actually got it started and moving, but I couldn't find the brakes and pinned my Tennessee friend against a pillar. He wasn't hurt, but I learned a few very descriptive curse words for my vocabulary.

Our stay in this building lasted for a few days, until we got our orders to move eastward and northward for the crossing of the Rhine River. This ended the famous phase of the crossing of the Roer. The phase had taken a long time. Although the distance from the Siegfried Line to the Roer River at Julich was only about seven miles, it had taken us over 4 months to travel this short distance and finally make the successful crossing. We had delays at the beginning, during which we took considerable time to prepare for the Roer crossing; we were interrupted for three months while we went down to fight the Battle of the Bulge; we had further delays when we got back, during which we spent additional time for additional training and building of supplies; and finally we were delayed another ten days when the Germans released the flood waters in the Roer.

At any rate, in the first part of March, 1945, we had successfully crossed the Roer, and we received orders to proceed to the point where we were assigned to cross the Rhine River. This point was located in the vicinity of Wesel, Germany.

Chapter 7 Pictures from Dan Smith's Album

Fig. 21 - Dan's Cronies in the Recon Patrol at the Crossing of the Roer

Fig. 22 - The entire 117th Recon Battalion - Crossing the Roer

Chapter 8

CROSSING THE RHINE RIVER
March 1945

Map 8A - Crossing the Rhine River

Chapter 8
CROSSING THE RHINE RIVER
March 1945

After successfully crossing the Roer River on February 23, 1945, we stayed for a brief period of time in our Regimental Headquarters near Julich, until the 30th Division was able to stabilize the new front that had been established by the crossing. This took about a week. We knew that our next step was to launch a crossing of the Rhine River, and that the crossing point was to be somewhere up north, near the town of Wesel, Germany, about 50 miles due north of Julich.

However, before heading directly up to the Wesel area, our 117th Regiment left Julich and proceeded to the area between Sittard and Echt, Holland, both of them adjacent to the Maas (Meuse) River. The Allied Command knew that the crossing of the Rhine was going to be a different experience than any of the prior river crossings, because the Rhine was so wide, and different equipment and techniques and procedures would be needed. What followed then was a three-week period of some of the most intensive training our Regiment had experienced since the beginning of our drive across Europe. Our engineers and regimental line units used the wide Maas River as a training place for the building of the bridges and practicing the use of various boats and vehicles that were to be used for the crossing of the wide Rhine.

This training took about two weeks, and then the Regiment received orders to proceed to the north and east to a town named Rayen, which was to be one of our assembly points for launching the crossing of the Rhine. The other assembly point was to be Wallach, Germany, about 10 miles north of Rayen, and at these points the intense training of the engineers and line units continued. In the meantime, my 117th Regimental patrol group (which had not participated in the training but had proceeded directly to the Wesel area) was allowed to go to the exact spot where the Rhine crossing was to be made, and we set up our observation points to provide continuing information to Regimental Headquarters with respect to terrain feature, the movement of enemy troops and artillery locations, and the like.

In the meantime, at Regimental Headquarters, as part of the training of our engineering and regimental units now located in Rayen and Wallach, an 8' by 8' sand table was built, detailing as much information as could be gathered about the terrain and about German positions and movement, wooded areas, and buildings. They used the information that we continuously fed them from our observation point, as well as information from scout planes flying over the area. A parade of regimental and squad leaders was brought in to be briefed about the terrain, obstacles, crossing sites and objectives of the crossing.

The plan of the crossing attack was for the 30th Division to concentrate on crossing along a six-mile line, stretching along the river from Wesel on the north to Mehrum on the south. The attack was to be three-pronged, with the 119th Division making the crossing in the north at a point in the southern suburbs of Wesel, the 120th Division attacking on the south, near Mehrum, and our 117th Division carrying the main burden of crossing in the center, near the small town of Ork. The Rhine is a very wide river, and at our crossing point it was estimated to be 1,100 feet, although it looked like a full mile. Other elements of Allied Forces were scheduled to make coordinated attacks across the Rhine at points both north of our six-mile line, and also south of us.

By March 18th, the intense training was coming to an end.

Taking a clue about the value of deception gained in our experiences in the River Roer crossings, the same kind of deceptive measures were practiced and enhanced while our 30th Division was making its final preparations at Rayen and Wallach. All members of the Division removed their shoulder patches, and vehicle markings were obliterated. A deception force of special troops wearing 30th Division shoulder patches, with 30th Division vehicle bumper markings moved down to a crossing point far to the south of our designated line, and false radio messages were sent indicating that the 30th was to cross at that point. Special roads that we built in our crossing area were duplicated up and down the the line outside our area, and if we sent out patrols in our area, similar patrols were sent out in other places along the line.

From my forward observation point near the Ork section, I could see that there was a dike along the east bank of the river. Beyond that, the land was flat and open for about two miles. Beyond that there was a high railroad embankment running parallel to the river, and about 1,000 yards beyond that was another similar railroad embankment. Even further beyond them was forest. There were very few buildings because this area was south of the southern limits of Wesel.

The launch of the crossing started just after midnight on March 24th. As a quick preview, I should say that the crossing was a huge success, and our Regiment made it across the Rhine completely on schedule, with no casualties and with no resistance from the Germans. The operation was a tribute to the value of careful, detailed preparation, coupled with strategic deceptiveness and a growing weakness of the German military.

To describe the crossing in more detail, on the evening of March 23rd, the foot troops of our Regiment were brought into the approaches to the launch site and took positions behind buildings or in any other hiding places that were available. At the same time, the engineers and the Navy and Marine personnel brought their boats and other crossing vehicles down and concealed them near the edge of the water on the west shore of the river. The word got around that Generals Eisenhower and Simpson were actually in the area at this point, riding through the approach roads and talking to the assembling foot troops as they moved toward the river. Although I did not see the Generals, the news brought home to us the importance of this operation.

At 1:00 a.m. on the 24th, our Allied artillery started a massive artillery barrage directed in the beginning at the eastern shore of the river and then gradually moving progressively inland. It involved laying thousands of rounds of high explosives and smoke on the east shore. I have heard it described as the greatest artillery barrage ever seen or heard. The east shore of the river was ablaze with fire and smoke. I did not participate in directing this artillery fire because it was area bombing rather than specific target bombing. As previously mentioned, I directed only target bombing.

After one hour of this saturation of the east shore, the artillery fire was shifted to deeper targets, and at this point our assault troops were given the word to launch the crossing. At this point, across the River from Ork, our engineers did not attempt to provide any bridges or treadways for the crossing. Everything was done with boats or barges or other vehicles that could navigate on the water, such as the new Alligators that were provided. We were aware that the engineers were in fact constructing a major bridge to the south of us, near Mehrum, but we did not see the bridge from our location.

When the assault started, our front line troop soldiers ran down to the water's edge, where all sorts of boats (assault boats, storm boats, and the like) were lined up on the slope of the dike leading down to the water. The troops had to grab these boats and drag them down to the water and then get in them and start across the river. The boats were motorized and Navy men were in charge of operating the motors and navigating across to the opposite shore. Sometimes the motors would not start right away, and the sailor would take some bantering until he finally succeeded.

A fleet of Alligators was available for carrying the troops across, and they turned out to be one of the most effective means of transportation for this crossing. Alligators were a new breed of vehicle that had been used in the Pacific War Theater and had recently been introduced into the European Theater. They were open troop carriers capable of navigating on land or water. They looked something like a tank and were equipped with fins on their treads. They were designed to carry about 24 fully equipped soldiers.

The crossing in a motorized boat or Alligator took about ten minutes. The operation proceeded on schedule and the first battalions of 117th Infantry soldiers reached the far shore and climbed up the dike and arrived in the town of Ork within about one-half hour after the launch of the attack. Other elements of the 117th followed in a steady stream. The troops arriving on the far shore were guided by machine gun tracer flares that marked the assembly points for each of the individual units, all according to plan. Once the units arrived at these points, they moved inland and had difficulty with visibility because of the layer of heavy smoke that our artillery had laid down, but they nevertheless proceeded on schedule.

Following the transportation of troops, there was a steady stream of supplies and equipment across the River. The Allied High Command was happy and satisfied with the manner in which the operation was conducted. Plenty of boats were available for transporting the troops and supplies. The supplies themselves kept arriving when needed. Ammunition and gasoline were in plentiful reserve.

I myself was transported across on a barge after most of the troops were across, and my jeep came along on a later barge. I did not encounter any resistance from the enemy in the entire crossing, and, to my knowledge, neither did any of the other elements of the 117th Regiment. As indicated earlier, the crossing at Ork was a huge success.

However, during the next few days, as we pushed eastward away from the Rhine, we found the progress to be slower and more difficult. After crossing the Rhine to Ork, it was calculated that if we could immediately push forward and secure the area between Ork and Dorsten, which was 20 miles to the east, we would have secured the crossing of the Rhine in our sector. This drive turned out to be more difficult than the actual crossing of the Rhine. We actually encountered spotty enemy resistance, roadblocks and minefields, as well as terrain problems that slowed us down considerably.

Our first objective was to reach and capture the town of Gahlen, which was about 12 miles east of Ork. The progress toward Gahlen at first was fairly easy, but when we entered the forest areas leading into Gahlen, the difficulties began. It was a dense forest, with muddy, unmarked roads and very hilly terrain where it was easy to get lost. Moreover, this is where we encountered our first effective counterattacks from the enemy. Previous to this, after leaving Ork we had run into occasional scattered, disorganized enemy machine gun fire, which could readily be knocked out, but the enemy counterattack in Gahlen forests was much different. In a move that was a surprise to us, the German High Command had brought in its crack 116th Panzer Division (which had been operating far to the north) and committed it to oppose our 30th Division. Some of this opposition took place in the forest around Gahlen. It was a great strain on our 117th Regiment to fight experienced German Panzer troops in a terrain such as this, where it was almost impossible to see the enemy, and very difficult to move our vehicles and troops without being mired in the muddy roads, and with enemy fire coming at our troops from every direction.

This combat in the Gahlen forest is etched in my memory. I will never forget it. I experienced more fright there than in any other part of our entire time in Europe. Were we scared? You betcha. As mentioned, in the depths of the forest, we were trying to get through to Gahlen, but most of the time we were lost and under terrific fire from the skilled Panzer troops. By this time, all our vehicles were mired in mud. We were totally on foot. We would hide behind trees, and again and again we would try to figure out when to run forward to the next tree. Thank God, we finally won the Gahlen Forest battle. When the war was finally over, three months later, and when I finally got back to the United States, I was known as a World War II veteran who did not talk very much about his adventures, but the battle in the Gahlen Forest was an exception. I remember talking about it to my family and friends right away and repeatedly through the following 65 years, even to the present day. It was and is my way of citing an example of what war is like.

Besides the harrowing experiences described above, another challenging factor took hold of us at this point: Sheer fatigue! Our Division's assault troops had been on the attack day and night for three full days, starting with the midnight launch of the Rhine crossing on March 24th, and with little or no rest and no hot meals. However, we persevered and, with the help of other 30th Division regiments, defeated the Panzer forces at that point.

It was an important victory, and the enemy lost significant numbers of its crack Panzer Division – all of which made the going for the 30th Division much easier for the rest of the war. With all these factors, the battle in the Gahlen forest area will always be a very unpleasant memory for our 117th Regiment's soldiers.

With this battle successfully behind us, our 117th Regiment entered the town of Gahlen, and although there was some routine street fighting with scattered enemy resistance, the town was soon captured. This was on March 27th. The way was now open for us to proceed eastward along the eight mile long highway toward our objective town, Dorsten. We occupied this town on March 29th without resistance, and were finally given three days of rest before resuming the drive across Germany to Berlin.

Chapter 8 Pictures
from Dan Smith's Album

Fig. 23 - Dan Smith and his Recon Patrol Buddies at the Crossing of the Rhine

Chapter 9

END OF THE WAR
April 1945

110 *Daniel D. Smith - Memoirs of World War II*

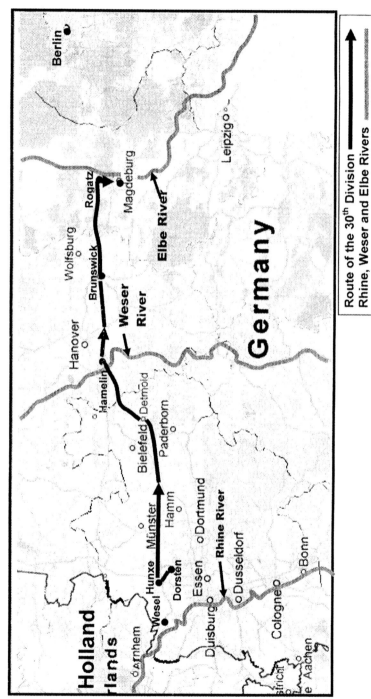

Map 9A - End of the War

Chapter 9
END OF THE WAR
April 1945

On March 27, 1945, having accomplished its goal of crossing the Rhine and securing the town of Dorsten, our 117th Regiment was given a three-day rest, waiting for its orders to proceed with the upcoming "rat-race" across Germany towards Berlin. When the orders finally came, the members of the 117th were delighted to hear that they had been assigned to partner with their favorite running mate, the 2nd Armored Division, for the drive across Germany. On April 1st the 117th dropped back to the town of Hunxe, where it joined forces with the 2nd Armored and started toward the town of Hamelin, which was about 145 miles to the northeast.

At this point the members of our 117th were in high spirits. Quartermaster supply lines were working with great efficiency. Contrasted with the drive across France, Belgium and Holland back in August and September of 1944, when shortages of gas and other supplies held up progress, this time was different. Our 117th had full gas tanks and rolling fuel reserves following behind. Besides this, the Quartermaster had added additional truck companies, and the line troops no longer had to walk. They were all motorized and were capable of moving 100 or more miles a day, contrasted with the 24 miles per day while walking. On top of all this, the news on the radio was that the German resistance was cracking everywhere.

The plan of partnership with the 2nd Armored involved the 2nd Armored taking the lead in pushing the front eastward, with the 30th Division handling the mopping up in their wake. This kind of duty meant a change in function for 30th Division. In addition to retaining its main function of fighting and driving forward, it now had the function of handling and guarding and feeding the liberated prisoners of war who were coming in streams from the east, heading west. It also had the function of guarding a variety of installations that were overrun – airports, ordnance shops, training camps, hospitals, etc. The 30th Division Surgeon found himself in charge of close to 10,000 German soldiers in military hospitals. I am not sure how our Division handled all of this extra burden, but I presume that our Quartermasters were able to beef up their personnel and supplies to meet the needs.

The first day, after leaving Hunxe, the 2nd Armored moved ahead very quickly without incident until it reached the area of the Teutoberger Wald (Forest) about a hundred miles to the east of Hunxe. The Teutoberger Wald has a mountainous ridge running roughly from the north to the south, with very few passes through the ridge. All these passes were being actively defended by local German militia troops and tanks. Different units of Allied forces were attempting to get through these various passes, and there were very vigorous battles up and down the line of the ridge for a period of three or four days. The Allied forces finally forced their way through the opposition. The 2nd Armored was able to get through the pass at the town of Detmold and was able to capture the town on April 4th. Our 117th Regiment followed closely in their rear, mopping up as we went.

The next day, April 5th, the 2nd Armored raced eastward for 25 miles to the city of Hamelin, located on the Weser River, with little or no opposition. The 2nd Armored secured the three bridges that cross the river, and encircled the city, but did not want to be delayed by going into the city and clearing it, so they continued on their drive to the east, leaving it to our 30th Division to enter the city and take whatever time was needed to secure it. This took us two or three days, and the mopping up was not difficult. Any German soldiers who were in the city were more interested in surrendering than fighting. All you had to do was fire your pistol into the air and a dozen Germans would appear, wanting to surrender.

During our two or three day stay, we had some time to become acquainted with this legendary city. Hamelin is very well known for its connection to the fable of the Pied Piper of Hamelin who, several centuries ago, was said to have cleared the city of rats by playing his pipe and attracting the rats and leading them out of the city and drowning them in the Weser River. In fact, while we were there in the city, one of the news reporters from the States

Ch. 9 - End of the War

organized a short skit in which some of our GI's got dressed up as rats and were led out of the city by a piper dressed up like the Pied Piper. The reporter took pictures of all this and sent them back home.

Another thing that we found out about Hamelin was that it is a well-known center for fine wines. Just about every home in the city had a wine cellar with substantial collections of elegant wines. Some of our guys collected a lot of these bottles of wine and put them on a half-ton Army trailer to take with us. This turned out to be a bad idea because when we got back on the road the trailer kept getting in the way of our rush to the east, and we finally just had to abandon it altogether, on the side of the road.

On April 8th our Division left Hamelin and drove eastward to catch up to the 2nd Armored which had already crossed the Leine River just south of the city of Hanover. The next mission was to capture the city of Brunswick, which is about 35 miles east of Hanover, and from that point drive on the to Elbe River. Two or three miles west of Brunswick there were a series of canals running in a north and south direction. Our 117th Regiment and other Allied forces units reached the canals on April 9th and were successful in crossing the canals and setting up an attack ring around the city. At this point Allied intelligence had received information that the German officers in command of Brunswick might be persuaded to surrender without any further battles, and in fact a meeting was arranged between our General Hobbs and the general in command of the city. However, the German general refused to accept the unconditional surrender terms offered by General Hobbs, and the Allied forces launched the attack on the city from all directions. After three days the city had fallen to the Allies, the Burgomeister had committed suicide, and the German general in command of the city had been captured.

I remember entering Brunswick after it fell, but our unit stayed there for only a couple of days because we were in a hurry. However, while we were there, I remember that some of our guys went into the Brunswick police department and found 60 Lugers and put them in my jeep. The Lugers covered the whole floor of the jeep. I was uncomfortable with this because I was pretty sure that there would be a search for them, so the next morning I turned them in.

Our 117th Regiment left one of its Battalions behind to mop up in the city of Brunswick, and the rest of us, together with the 2nd Armored and other Allied units, raced 35 miles eastward, with only negligible resistance, and reached the Elbe River on April 13th. My Reconnaissance Patrol Unit and other elements of our 117th Regiment came down to the river at the City of Rogatz, approximately 14 miles north of the City of Magdeburg.

The original plans had been for our Regiment to cross the Elbe at Rogatz and continue on for the 45 miles to reach Berlin. I remember sitting in my jeep, poised to cross the bridge of the River with my Patrol group of six jeeps, with a map of the suburbs of Berlin in my lap, and wondering "It's a big place for only six jeeps." However, right at that point, we received orders from Headquarters to stop. They held us for 20 minutes, and then 15 minutes, and then another 20 minutes, and then they told us that this was as far east as we were going. The word had come that the Russians had reached Berlin, and the political strategy between the Russian and Allied High Commands was for the Allied forces to stay west of the Elbe and leave it to the Russians to capture and mop up in Berlin. Our objective was changed. It was now to solidify our control of the front along the west side of the Elbe River. This meant that we were not to cross the Elbe but rather to turn south and drive the 14 miles to Magdeburg, which was on the west side of the Elbe, and to participate in capturing Magdeburg, which was a major crossroads and bridgehead on the Elbe.

The drive down the west side of the Elbe toward Magdeburg was not without incident. The same day we left Rogatz, we came across a train parked on an abandoned siding near the town of Farsleben, with hundreds of people sitting and standing in the fields surrounding the train. Although we did not know at the time who these people were, we could see that they were emaciated and in poor physical condition. We could not stop because we were on a fast track to Magdeburg, but we sent word to 30th Division

Headquarters that there was a situation here that had to be handled. We later found out that this was a trainload of about 2,500 Jews who had been taken from the Nazi concentration camp at Bergen Belsen and forced on to a train and taken on a wandering train ride across northern Germany, as the Nazis tried to get them to a camp where they could be eliminated before the Americans or Russians caught up with them. Since the prisoners had little food, many of them died on this wandering journey. As the end of the war approached, the train happened to be in the vicinity of Magdeburg, and it was shunted into this little unimportant valley siding near Farsleben and abandoned. This is where we discovered them on our drive from Rogatz to Magdeburg. We heard later that, when 30th Division Headquarters got the message from us, they sent rescue units who took charge of the Jews and fed them and cared for them and put them on trains heading back to the English Channel, where many of them were taken on ships to the United States and later became citizens.

As we moved southward from Farsleben on our drive toward Magdeburg, we came to a point where there were some small cottages grouped together on the west side of the road. We stopped and went over there and went into one of the cottages, and immediately somebody out in the back yard started shooting at us with rifles through the windows. I got one of our guys to shoot a mortar shell straight up in the air so that it would land in the back yard, and when this happened there was a lot of scrambling in the back yard and the rifle fire stopped. However, when we went back to the road and got in our vehicles, the rifle shots started again. We could see then that the group of cottages was a school, and out in front of the school a teacher was teaching his students how to fire at us. I had my machine gun on my jeep, and I could have easily mowed them down, but I did not. I did not want to shoot at kids.

As we proceeded further down the road we caught up with some of our tanks and fell in behind them. We soon came to a tributary river that was flowing from the west into the Elbe. There was a bridge over the tributary, that we needed to cross, but the tanks did not want to cross because they could see four German soldiers down under the bridge, who looked like they were ready to blow the bridge. A couple of us in our jeeps took a running start and raced across the bridge, and then discovered that the four soldiers down there were dead. So the tanks proceeded across.

I went back across the bridge to take one last look, and while I was on the bridge a German officer suddenly appeared on my seat next to me. He said he wanted to surrender, and he had surrender papers in his brief case. However, I quickly found out that he was a phony. He was not an officer. His officer's uniform was phony, and he didn't have any surrender papers. I got him out of the jeep and drove on.

On April 13th, when we arrived at the northern edge of the city of Magdeburg, we were joined there by other units of our 117th Regiment and by units of the 2nd Armored. Also, other Allied forces units had moved to the west edge of the city, and additional units had moved up from the south to occupy the south edge of the city. At this point, with Allied forces established on the north, west, and south perimeters and with Magdeburg hemmed in by the Elbe River on the east, with all its bridges broken, the attack on Magdeburg was ready to begin. Here again, there was an attempt to negotiate a surrender of the city, but this did not happen, and the attack began. It was preceded by heavy aerial bombing from Allied bombers, and then the ground forces moved in from all sides and fought their way into Magdeburg. The enemy resistance was troublesome but not intense. It consisted of roadblocks built around machine guns and antitank guns, mostly around the outer perimeter of the city, as well as snipers and some makeshift obstacles such as trolley cars and wagons filled with dirt. The Allied forces swept through these and within 24 hours captured the city. This was on April 18th.

At this point the 30th Division's fighting career in Europe ended, and the 30th became the administrator of a military government over a city that was in turmoil. There was civilian mob looting in the streets. There were thousands of German soldiers trying to surrender. There was the job of taking over and handling and caring for thousands of prisoners (slave laborers, Russian soldiers, etc.) previously held captive by the German Army. There was also the job of guarding many different kinds of locations that were subject to looting, such as food warehouses, liquor stores, factories, and even banks. The Headquarters officers were swamped with the responsibility of dealing with all these things, in addition to militarily governing the conduct of a large city's daily affairs. The officers did not have time to give out specific orders to the platoons of Allied soldiers who had come into the city, and the soldiers were pretty much left to their own judgment as to which of the protective duties they should perform.

My own reconnaissance platoon of 20 men stayed together and tended to assume various guard duties as the need arose in different parts of the city. I remember that on one occasion, a man came up to us and took us to a low, one-story building, by the river, in a small square. He took some of our guys down in the basement. I did not go because I had to stay with my jeep which had the big machine gun. When our guys came back they reported that the basement was loaded with German money. We put a guard on the place – not right there, but at a distance, so that nobody would notice it. Three days later 17 English Army lorries showed up and hauled all the money away. We had a lot of discussion among ourselves as to who really owned money like that. At any rate, in this case, the English got it, and it didn't fall into the hands of looters.

After a few days of dealing with the confusion and turmoil in Magdeburg, my platoon decided that we needed to make ourselves a little more comfortable, and we took over an apartment building in the city. On the outskirts, we found a railroad car containing a load of generators, and we took these back to the apartment to provide us with power for making our stay a little more livable.

After about three weeks of dealing with the churning events in Magdeburg, we still had not seen any sign of any Russian soldiers. We knew they had captured Berlin about 45 miles east of us and were heading our way, but they seemed to be taking their time. Finally, on May 6th, the Russians showed up on the east bank of the Elbe River, and the Russian general in command of the Red Army division crossed the river and had lunch with our commanding general, General Hobbs. This was designated as the official meeting of the Allied and Russian armies.

The next day, May 7th, news came to us over the wires that the war in Europe had ended. May 8th was designated as the official day for celebrating the war's end.

For the next two or three weeks, our 30th Division stayed in the Magdeburg area, serving as a military government. During that time, to my knowledge none of our Allied soldiers crossed over the river to mingle with the Russians, and very few Russians came across to Magdeburg to mingle with our soldiers. There were, however, some exceptions. I was aware that at one point a small group of Russian officers came across and had a luncheon (with vodka cocktails) with some of our officers. The thing that I remember is that they had plentiful supplies of American money. The word got out that our U.S. Treasury, in some negotiations with the Russian High Command, had provided the Russians with U.S. currency printing plates, and the Russians had actually printed large quantities of US money. The Russian officers who came across had a lot of this money and wanted to spend it. Specifically, they wanted to buy American uniforms, or anything else of that nature, from our officers and enlisted men. Some of our men actually sold their stuff and got the money. I tried to discourage the men in our unit from doing this, because I took the position that it was counterfeit money. However, this didn't make me very popular with our soldiers. Some of our men took these US dollars and drove down to Austria and bought a truck load of beer, which they brought back to our headquarters.

During our stay in the Magdeburg area, the Allied Military Government was faced with the major problem of handling the thousands of German soldiers who were surrendering in droves. The German soldiers were deathly afraid of being captured by the Russians, whom they regarded as cruel and ruthless. The Germans who were surrendering to us came not only from the inner city of Magdeburg, but also in large numbers from locations on the east side of the river. They came across on broken bridges, on boats, and some of them even tried to swim. There were stories of luckless

Ch. 9 - End of the War

Germans being caught swimming and being machine gunned by the Russians. Our Allied Command tried to cope with this major flow of prisoners by setting up three or four prisoner of war camps in the western suburbs of Magdeburg.

Toward the end of this period we got a chance to see and talk to a Russian officer and a small group of enlisted men who had been given the assignment to bring a Russian encampment of prisoners over the river to a point in the northern suburbs of Magdeburg. The prisoners were captured German soldiers as well as slave laborers from Germany and Poland. The Russian officer apparently had the assignment to get rid of these prisoners one way or another because they were too much of a burden for the Russian Army. The Officer first went about this by giving knapsacks to selected numbers of the prisoners and telling them to hike back to Poland or Berlin or Moscow or wherever they came from. However, because he could not get rid of all of them in this way, for various reasons, he still had a large number of prisoners camped on top of a hill. He got in touch with an Allied officer and asked if the Allies would take the prisoners off his hands. The Allied command agreed, and I was part of a group who took 15 trucks up to that hill and loaded up these trucks to the point we thought we were going to break some prisoners' arms and legs and ribs. We drove the trucks, with tires popping, to the prisoner of war camps that the Allies had set up in the western suburbs. In the camp, the prisoners had to be fed, deloused, and otherwise cared for. The next day we heard that the Russian officer was shot for letting us take the prisoners off his hands. I have no idea why he was considered by the Russian Command to have done something wrong???

My limited experience with Russian officers and men told me that they were indeed cruel and ruthless and somewhat obnoxious, and I was not surprised that they were feared by the Germans. It is interesting to look back and realize that this fear was what motivated the German High Command in some of the strategic and political moves it made toward the end of the war, starting with the Battle of the Bulge, where the German objective was to gain enough bargaining power to be able to surrender to the Allies rather than the Russians. Finally, at the end of this period, one last mission was assigned to me. The mission arose out the fact that, in the period just prior to the end of the War, Magdeburg and its oil refineries had been bombed extensively, and also, during the capture of Magdeburg, extensive additional aerial bombing was done, all of this leaving large parts of the city in ruin, and also leaving a dangerous number of unexploded artillery shells scattered throughout the city.

Our officers were contacted by the German Burgomaster of the City, who complained, in the first place, about how unnecessary the bombing attacks against his city had been, with the end of the War being so close, and in the second place asking what the US Army was going to do about all the artillery shell duds that had been left behind. The officers of our regiment agreed to do the job of disposing of them, and I was the one that was chosen to do it. I was provided with three trucks and three unhappy men and was told that I was in command, but with no rating.

The Burgomaster had supplied a list showing the location of all known dud shells in the city, and we set out to carry out the mission. It had been arranged to have the disposal operation take place in a farmer's small quarry near a farmhouse at the outskirts of the City. As we visited places on the list, we found shells in all manner of places – in shops, in homes, in basements, and even displayed on fireplace mantels. In addition, in one of the railway yards of the city, we found a box car full of 40 mm anti-aircraft shells that were still unexploded, even though the box car had been split in two by fighter bombers. Everything that we found we loaded into the three trucks, and repeated trips were made out to the quarry.

As the final operation, I kept one man, and the two of us went out to the quarry and made three large piles of the shells and set the fuses, and then we lit the fuses and RAN away into the nearby field where we had parked our truck. To our dismay, as we ran, a small artillery spotter plane showed up, heading for the vicinity of the quarry, and he refused to leave despite all our waving and yelling. He was over the bombs when they detonated. A large amount of iron came down on us, and we saw the plane go up and disappear in a cloud, and we never found out what happened to it. I hope he made it. Also, to this day, I wonder if the farmhouse itself was damaged. The detonation had thrown the iron much farther then we had expected.

This was the end of our stay in Magdeburg. On May 27th, 1945, British troops moved in and occupied Magdeburg, and our 117th Infantry moved southward to begin its mission of somehow or other getting back home. See the next Chapter.

Chapter 9 Pictures
from Dan Smith's Album

Fig. 24 - Dan Smith Being Awarded the Bronze Star for his part in the 117th Regiment's motorized drive across Germany to the Elbe River. Dan was a member of the intelligence and reconnaissance platoon which spearheaded the drive. His Bronze Star Citation stated that Dan's "outstanding courage and devotion to duty were a source of inspiration to his comrades," particularly during the extraordinarily heavy resistance that was met on the drive from Brunswick to the Elbe on April 10th to 13th, 1945.

Fig. 25 - First Meeting of US and Russian Soldiers in Magdeberg

Fig. 26 - Round-up of Prisoners Being Turned Over By Russians To 30th Division for Trucking to 30th's Prison Camp

Fig. 27 - Russians' Prisoners Being Trucked to 30th Division's Prison Camp

Fig. 28 - Russians' Prisoners Being Trucked to 30th Division's Prison Camp

Fig. 29 – Russian Prisoners Who Have Been Released in Magdeburg and Told To Walk Back Home

Fig. 30 - Russians' Prisoners Who Have Been Released in Magdeburg and Told to Walk Back Home

Fig. 31 - Allied Aerial Bombing Just Before the End of the War Left Magdeburg in Shambles

Fig. 32 - Showing the Damage to Magdeburg

Fig. 33 - Searching for Dud Aerial Bombs

Fig. 34 - Dud Aerial Bombs Collected from the Magdeburg Aria, Ready for Detonation

Chapter 10

GOING HOME
May 1945 - September 1945

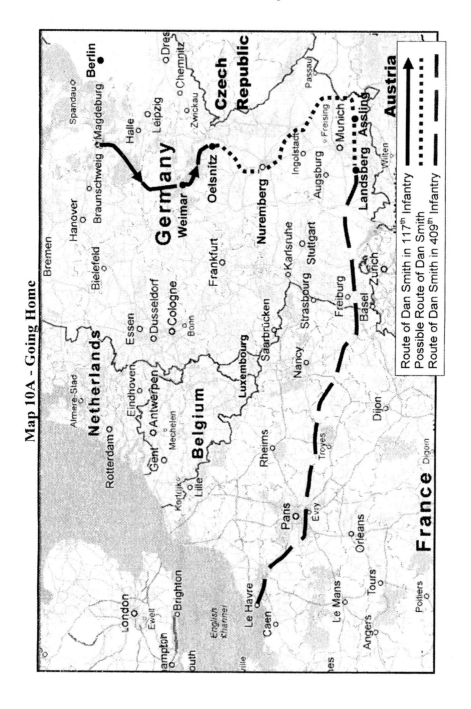

Map 10A - Going Home

Chapter 10

GOING HOME
May 1945 - September 1945

Our stay in Magdeburg ended on May 27th, 1945, when British troops moved in and took over the occupation of the town. Our 117th Infantry then moved about 150 miles south to the vicinity of Oelsnitz, Germany, near the Csechoslovakian border, for occupation of the area.

On the way down to Oelsnitz, we stopped in the town of Weimar, Germany, and made a visit to the Buchenwald concentration camp nearby. Buchenwald was a Nazi concentration camp that had been established in 1938 and held over 240,000 prisoners during the years until it was liberated in April of 1945 – just one month before we arrived there. The camp had held prisoners from all over Europe (Jews, religious and political prisoners, criminals, homosexuals, and prisoners of war). Although it was not technically an extermination camp, it has been estimated that over 56,000 prisoners died there, either by execution or by starvation, illness, or by being overworked to death. Many of the prisoners had been used for human experimentation and died in the development of vaccines or weapons of death. When we arrived, most of the prisoners had been taken away by the Allies, but we did see a few remaining, emaciated prisoners who were still there. We saw the barracks where the starving prisoners were held in overcrowded, stenching conditions, and we saw the crematorium and the graveyards where so many dead prisoners had been disposed of.

After leaving Buchenwald, we proceed to Oelsnitz, and, shortly after we got there, orders were received that the 30th Division was to be redeployed back to the United States and then to the Pacific Theater of Operation for the Japanese War. Our stay in the Oelsnitz area was for an extended period, and during this period many things were happening. There was a point system in place, under which each man was assigned a certain number of points, depending on how long he had been in the service, what kind of service he had performed, how many medals he had received, etc., etc. Men with the highest number of points were to be transferred back to the US first, and for this purpose men were being transferred and exchanged back and forth between various divisions and infantry units, under a system that was not always easy to understand. I myself was transferred at least three different times, so I did not remain with the 117th Regiment. During the time when men were waiting for their number to come up, they were assigned to various occupation duties.

The duty I was chosen for was to serve as a military guard on one after another of the many trains that were operating in the region. The train situation was very confused. Troop trains, freight trains, passenger trains and prisoner trains of all kinds were moving in every direction. The trains were moving during the day and also at night, without lights. For my guard duty, I would be sitting in the cab of the engine with the engineer and fireman, neither of whom spoke English. I myself knew nothing about trains. This kind of thing went on for over a month.

Finally, some time in July of 1945, I was riding in one of these trains and the engineer and the fireman became excited, because they could see a light reflection on the track ahead of us, telling them that another train was on the track ahead of us. We couldn't see the train itself, but the light reflection told them that there was going to be a crash. **So I jumped off the train!!** I have no memory of what happened after that. I do not know if the trains crashed. I have no idea how long my memory loss lasted. All I remember is that I later found myself on a farm outside the town of Landsberg, Germany, a southwestern suburb of Munich. I was being fed and cared for by the farmer.

> As mentioned, I have no memory as to whether the two trains crashed after I jumped off. In recent years, I have done some research and have found that there was indeed a train crash on July 16th, 1945, near the German town of Assring, a southeastern suburb of

Munich. The crash is well-documented in newspaper reports of the period, and there are monuments in nearby cities memorializing the crash. It appears that a US freight train carrying US tanks had crashed into a passenger train that had been stalled on the track ahead of it. The passenger train had been carrying German prisoners of war who were being transported back to their homeland to be discharged. 116 of the prisoners were killed in the crash and many more injured.

The US freight train in the Assring wreck may have been the one I jumped from. I cannot say this for sure. There were so many other trains running in that area at that time. On the other hand, the date and place of the Assring wreck are consistent with where I could have been at the time. If indeed the train in the Assring wreck was the one I jumped from, then the good Lord was watching over me when I jumped off a train and escaped a wreck in which over 100 men were killed.

I do remember that I was with the farmer near Landsberg for several weeks. I also remember that he told me that Landsberg was a prison town with an important place in German history. The Landsberg Prison was where Adolf Hitler was imprisoned in 1925 in the days of his youth, and it was where he wrote his book, *Mein Kampf.*

Except for these few straggling snatches of memories, there is not much else that I remember about the stay on the farm, as I was trying to get my mind back together again.

Finally, I do remember that one day a US Army Officer showed up on the farm and asked me who I was and what I was doing there. He was an officer with the 409th Infantry Regiment which had been in Innsbruck, Austria, when the war ended, and which was now moving westward, through Landsberg, on its way to Le Havre, to board a ship for the US. Apparently somebody in the town had told him that there was an American soldier living on a farm outside the town, so he came looking for me. He told me to join the 409th and go back to the US with them.

On August 24th, the 409th left Landsberg, and I went with them to Le Havre, and then, after further processing at Le Havre, we sailed for the United Sates on September 9th, 1945. Our ship arrived in New York Harbor and sailed past the Statue of Liberty at 2 a.m. in total silence. Everybody on board was asleep, but I found myself on the deck, watching what was happening. We sailed up the River to Fort Dix. Some very nice older women came aboard in the morning and gave us each little cartons of chocolate milk.

From New York, I was sent to Fort Sheridan, Illinois, just north of Chicago, my home town. My discharge papers show that I was discharged at Fort Sheridan on September 27, 1945, as a member of the 409th Infantry. I took the good old North Shore train back down to Chicago and arrived at my home, only to find that nobody was home. However, my mother soon arrived, and then my father, and then the rest of my family, **and I was home.**

Although I was technically a member of the 409th Infantry when I was discharged, substantially all of my career during the war was obviously as a member of the 117th Regiment of the 30th Division. I got separated from the 117th at the very end of the war, while we were in the Oelsnitz area, where the point system was causing men to be transferred and exchanged back and forth between regiments and divisions, but in fact and in deed, and deep in my heart, I was, and still consider myself to be, a proud member of the 117th Regiment.

The records show that, in late July, 1945, the 117th Regiment, as part of the 30th Division, left the Oelsnitz area and moved to Le Havre, France, and then crossed the English Channel and started embarking on the Queen Mary for transportation back to the U.S.A., from where they were to be redeployed to the Pacific Theater of War. At this point, because of all the transferring and exchanging of personnel that had gone on in the Oelsnitz area, most of the officers and men who had fought through the war with me had been transferred out, leaving almost entirely different personnel who had just recently been transferred into the Regiment. At any rate, while they were embarking on the Queen Mary, news of the Japanese surrender was received and redeployment plans were cancelled. The 117th was just going home.

The career and reputation of the 117th Regiment and the 30th Division was illustrious. We were in combat almost a year. Our regimental headquarters moved 85 times, and 650 miles. We were in 5 major battles. Our normal regimental strength was about 1,400. We had 4,685 casualties and 717 dead. Total casualties returned to the unit were 1,527.

I was continuously amazed at the achievements of our line companies. To all of them I give all the credit, to all the combat infantry men everywhere, and to our officers. The officers were our leaders, and 294 of them were casualties in our unit. Our Regiment and Division had become respected and feared by the enemy. We shattered their best forces at the Siegfried Line and again in the Battle of the Bulge, and again at many other places during the long drive across Europe.

For my part, when I arrived back in Chicago and was able to resume my life, I looked back and thanked God for looking over me during those war years. At the end, I was still a private, ***but still alive.*** We had won the war. We had fought with full support of the entire US nation behind us, not only in material things but in spirit and sincere confidence that this was a significant and worthwhile war. I had my whole life ahead of me. I married Mary Louise, the love of my life, and we had five children.. I participated in the glorious advances of business, government and technology in our nation in the 1950s and succeeding years. I have been able to work with and watch and encourage my Baby Boomer family, and many other Baby Boomers, to take hold and help develop this nation into the outstanding technological and economic power that it has become over the past 60 years.

Chapter 10 Pictures
from Dan Smith's Album

Fig. 35 - On the Way Home, A Visit to Buchenwald. This is The Entrance

Fig. 36 - One of the Guard Towers at Buchenwald Prison

Fig. 37 - The Crematory at Buchenwald, Showing the Electric Guard Fence

Fig. 38 - More Electric Guard Fencing and Another Tower

Ch. 10 - Going Home 139

Fig. 39 - The Buchenwald Furnace

Fig. 40 - Containers for Ashes from the Buchenwald Furnace

Fig. 41 - The Hanging Scaffold at Buchenwald

Fig. 42 - In the Foreground, One of the Buchenwald Prisoners, Still Lingering in the Prison

Fig. 43 - Oelsnitz, Germany, the Gathering Point Where Many US Divisions Waited for Their Turn to be Transferred Back to the US

Fig. 44 - Dan Smith, Whiling Away Hours in the Oelsnitz Area

Fig. 45 - Town Square in Town Near Oelsnitz

Fig. 46 - Railroad Yards in Nuremberg, Germany, Where Dan Was Assigned to Guard Duty on a Train

TIME TABLE

Daniel D. Smith's Service During World War II
1942-1945
30th Division, 117th Infantry Regiment

Date

Nov. 10
1942 — Enlisted in the United States Army in Chicago, Illinois and sent to Fort Sheridan, Illinois, to receive uniform and shots.

Nov. 11
1942 — Transported by train to Camp Blanding, Florida, to begin basic training. Was assigned to the cavalry reconnaissance and intelligence troop of the 30th Old Hickory Infantry Division (Andrew Jackson's old Division).

May
1943 — Moved to Camp Forrest, Tennessee, to begin six months of field maneuvers.

Nov.
1943 — Moved by truck to Camp Attebury, Indiana, for final preparations for overseas duty. Was transferred to the Recon and Intelligence Platoon of the 117th Regiment

Feb. 1944	Moved by train to Camp Myles Standish, Massachusetts, an overseas staging camp serving the Boston Port of Embarkation. Received another round of shots.
Feb. 12, 1944	Loaded on a transport ship and left Boston Harbor in a blinding snowstorm, as part of a troop convoy, headed across the northern Atlantic for England.
Feb. 22, 1944	Landed at Liverpool, England, and was transported by train to our initial training encampment in the southern part of England, near London.
June 6 1944	D-Day. The first wave of American, British and Canadian forces hit the Normandy beaches.
June 10 1944	D-Day+4. The 30th Division hit Omaha Beach.
July 6 1944	General Patton flew to Normandy, and his headquarters staff and eventually his 3rd Army began arriving on the Normandy beaches.

July 12 1944	30th Division designated as the lead unit in Operation Cobra, to spearhead the breakthrough at Saint Lo, thus allowing General Patton's Third Army to proceed southward to Brest.
July 24 1944	Bombed by the American 8th Air Force, in error, killing 25 men and wounding 131. Delayed jump off of Operation Cobra by one day.
July 25 1944	Bombed again, in error, by the 8th Air Force, killing 111 men, including Lt. General Leslie McNair, and wounding 490.
July 19 1944	Saint Lo was captured by the First Army, but the city remained under German fire, and the First Army's attempt to drive beyond the city ground to a stalemate.
July 25 1944	Operation Cobra took off, despite the two tragic friendly fire errors and losses.

Aug. 6-12
1944   Battle of Mortain. 2nd Battalion of the 120th Regiment surrounded on Hill #314 for five days. German High Command declared this battle to be the major turning point in the war, leading to the ultimate defeat of the German Army.

Aug. 14
1944   Started the "rat race" across northern France.

Aug. 23
1944   Evreux liberated.

Aug. 25
1944   Paris liberated.

Aug. 27
1944   Crossed the Seine River.

Sep. 1
1944   Entered Belgium.

Sep. 3
1944   Liberated Tournai, Belgium.

Sep. 10
1944   Crossed the Meuse River at Vise and Liege.

Sep. 12
1944   Entered Holland.

Time Table

Sep. 14 1944	Liberated Maastricht, Holland.
Oct. 2 1944	Attack on Siegfried Line at Aachen begins.
Oct. 16 1944	City of Aachen captured.
Dec. 17 1944	Beginning of 30th Division's participation in the Battle of the Bulge.
Jan. 30 1945	German breakthrough effort at Battle of the Bulge defeated.
Feb. 2 1945	30th Division returns to original River Roer position in Germany.
Feb. 23 1945	The River Roer was successfully crossed near Julich, Germany.
Mar. 1 1945	30th Division proceeded to places like Echt and Sittard, Holland, to use the Maas River to train for the upcoming crossing of the Rhine.
Mar. 18 1945	Proceeded to assembly area near Rayen.

Mar. 23 1945	Proceeded to assembly area near Wallach.
Mar. 24-27 1945	The Rhine River was successfully crossed near Wesel, Germany.
Mar. 27 1945	Defeated crack Panzer troops in the Gahlen Forest. Captured Gahlen.
Mar. 29 1945	Occupied the town of Dorsten.
Apr. 4 1945	Broke through the Teutoberger Wald mountain gap at the town of Detmold and captured the town.
Apr. 5-8 1945	Captured the city of Hamelin and spent three days in the city, mopping up.
Apr. 9-12 1945	Captured the city of Brunswick and spent three days in the city, mopping up.
Apr. 13 1945	Reached the Elbe River at the town of Rogatz (14 miles north of Magdeburg and 45 miles west of Berlin).

Apr. 13 1945	Arrived at northern edge of Magdeburg and prepared for the attack against the city.
April 16 1945	Start of the attack to capture Magdeburg.
Apr. 18 1945	Magdeburg was captured. The 30th Division started a 40-day period in which it acted as the military government of the captured city.
May 6 1945	First official contact with the Russian Army, now arriving in Magdeburg.
May 6 1945	Teletype message announcing the end of the war in Europe.
May 7 1945	Hostilities officially ceased.
May 28 1945	30th Division left Magdeburg, proceeding south to an area near Oelsnitz, Germany, to carry out occupation duties and prepare for redeployment.
May 29 1945	En route to Oelsnitz, visited Buchenwald Prison, near Weimar, Germany.

June 1945	At Oelsnitz, assigned to occupation duties (riding as armed guard on various transport trains) while waiting for points number to come up for return to US.
July 1945	Jumped off train to avoid train wreck and woke up on a farm near Landsberg, Germany, being cared for by the farmer.
Aug. 24 1945	Left Landsberg as a member of the 409th Infantry, bound for LeHavre, France, to board ship to the U.S.
Sep. 9 1945	Boarded transport ship at LeHavre and set sail for the U.S.
Sep. 19 1945	Sailed past the Statue of Liberty in New York Harbor and disembarked in New York City.
Sep. 21 1945	Traveled by train to Fort Sheridan, Illinois.
Sep. 27 1945	Received my discharge from the U.S. Army and took the train to my home in Chicago.

TABLE OF MAPS

Map No.		Page No.
	Master Map	xii
1A	*Life Before Going Overseas in World War II*	xiv
2A	*England - Assembly of Troops and Materials For the 1944 Invasion of the Continent*	18
3A	*Normandy - Landing on Omaha Beach and Battles Beyond*	26
4A	*Northwestern France - The Chase from Mortain to the Seine*	38
5A	*From Paris to the Siegfried Line*	47
5B	*Close-up of Siegfried Line Area*	48
6A	*The Battle of the Bulge*	67
6B	*Close-up of Malmedy Area*	68
7A	*Crossing the Roer River*	85
8A	*Crossing the Rhine River*	98
9A	*End of the War*	110
10A	*Going Home*	130

TABLE OF PICTURES

Fig. No.		Page No.
1	*The co-authors: Dan Smith and Frank Barber*	xi
2	*At the start of the Ozarks Trip: Frank Dubnick, John Dubnick, Dan Smith, Frank Barber*	5
3	*Dan as a Cyclist*	6
4	*Dan as a Soldier*	6
5	*Dan Smith at Basic Training Camp in Florida*	13
6	*Training in the Use of Wartime Weaponry*	14
7	*Troop Ship in Boston Harbor, waiting for 30th Division to Embark*	14
8	*30th Division Troops on Board, Ready for Start of the Transit to England*	15
9	*Dan Smith on Board, Ready to Start Transit to England*	15
10	*Recon Unit Scouting Belgian Countryside in Front of Advancing 117th Regiment*	61
11	*Another 117th Recon Unit in the Drive Across Belgium*	61
12	*Dan Smith With Kids in Belgian Village*	62

13	Dan Smith in Germany, Waiting for Orders to Crash the Siegfried Line	62
14	Dan Smith Being Awarded the Silver Star for Bravery in Reaching and Maintaining a Forward Observation Post Under Heavy Enemy Concentrations of Artillery Fire, and Providing Crucial Information that Enabled Piercing of the Siegfried Line.	63
15	Scouting Operations in the Snowy Malmedy Area	79
16	More Scouting Around Malmedy	79
17	Dan Smith in Position Above Stavelot	80
18	Dan in Position Above Stavelot	80
19	Dan in the Woods Above Stamelot	81
20	The Battle of the Bulge Was Fought in the Dead of Winter	81
21	Dan's Cronies in the Recon Patrol at the Crossing of the Roen	95
22	The Entire 117*th* Recon Battalion - Crossing the Roer	95
23	Dan Smith and His Recon Patrol Buddies at the Crossing of the Rhine.	107

Table of Pictures - Continued

24	Dan Smith Being Awarded the Bronze Star for his part in the 117th Regiment's motorized drive across Germany to the Elbe River. Dan was a member of the intelligence and reconnaissance platoon which spearheaded the drive. His Bronze Star Citation stated that Dan's "outstanding courage and devotion to duty were a source of inspiration to his comrades," particularly during the extraordinarily heavy resistance that was met on the drive from Brunswick to the Elbe on April 10th to 13th, 1945.	123
25	First Meeting of US and Russian Soldiers in Magdeberg	124
26	Round-up of Prisoners Being Turned Over By Russians to 30th Division for Trucking to 30th's Prison Camp	124
27	Russians' Prisoners Being Trucked to 30th Division's Prison Camp	125
28	Russians' Prisoners Being Trucked to 30th Division's Prison Camp.	125
29	Russians' Prisoners Who Have Been Released in Magdeberg and Told To Walk Back Home	126
30	Russians' Prisoners Who Have Been Released in Magdeberg and Told to Walk Back Home	126
31	Allied Aerial Bombing Just Before the End of the War Left Magdeberg in Shambles	127
32	Showing the Damage to Magdeberg	127

33	**Searching for Dud Aerial Bombs**	**128**
34	**Dud Aerial Bombs, Collected from the Magdeberg Area, Ready for Detonation**	**128**
35	**On the Way Home, A Visit to Buchenwald. This is the Entrance.**	**137**
36	**One of the Guard Towers at Buchenwald Prison**	**137**
37	**The Crematory at Buchenwald, Showing the Electric Guard Fence.**	**136**
38	**More Electric Guard Fencing &Another Tower**	**138**
39	**The Buchenwald Furnace**	**139**
40	**Containers for Ashes from the Buchenwald Furnace**	**139**
41	**The Hanging Scaffold at Buchenwald**	**140**
42	**In the Foreground, One of the Buchenwald Prisoners, still Lingering in the Prison.**	**140**
43	**Oelsnitz, Germany, the Gathering Point Where Many US Divisions Waited for Their Turn To Be Transferred Back to the US**	**141**
44	**Dan Smith, Whiling Away the Hours in the Oelswitz Area**	**141**
45	**Town Square in a Town Near Oelswitz**	**142**
46	**Railroad Yards in Nuremberg, Germany, Where Dan Was Assigned to Guard Duty on a Train**	

Index

1

116th Panzer, 104
117th Regiment, 10, 11, 42, 49, 51, 56, 61, 70, 76, 87, 89, 91, 99, 103, 104, 105, 111, 112, 113, 114, 116, 123, 132, 134, 135, 143, 153, 155
117th Regiment, Recon and Intelligence Platoon, 10, 32, 40, 143
119th Division, 100
120th Division, 100
1932 Olympics races, 2

2

23 miles, 39, 43, 51
29th Division, 27, 28
2nd Armored, 57, 111, 112, 113, 114, 116

3

30th Division, i, iii, ix, 8, 9, 10, 15, 19, 27, 32, 33, 35, 42, 49, 53, 55, 56, 70, 87, 91, 99, 100, 104, 105, 111, 112, 114, 116, 118, 124, 125, 131, 134, 135, 143, 144, 145, 147, 149, 153, 155, 163
30th Division Reconnaissance, 8
30th Division Surgeon, 111
30th Old Hickory Infantry Division, 8, 143

4

409th Infantry Regiment, 133, 134, 150
4th Division, 44

7

75th Division, 87, 92

A

Aachen, 53, 55, 56, 57, 58, 59, 69, 70, 87, 147
Ade, Harold, 2, 3, 4
aerial bombardment, 31, 33, 56, 116, 120
Africa, 10
Allied aircraft, 31, 33
Allied High Command, 41, 43, 55, 59, 87, 88, 103, 114
Alligator tanks, 89, 102
Alsdorf, 57, 58, 59, 69, 78
Ambleve River, 73, 74, 75
American B-26 bombers, 76
American General Hospital, 76
American High Command, 42
American money, 118
American P24's Friendly Fire, 33, 34, 42, 145
Americans, v, 115
Antwerp, 32, 50, 71, 72
Ardennes, 59, 70, 77
Ardennes Offensive, 59, 77
area bombing, 89, 102
Argentan, 42
Army Enlistment Center, 6
artillery barrage, 101
artillery fire, 9, 54, 55, 56, 75, 88, 102
artillery shell duds, 120
Assring, Germany, 132, 133
Atlantic, 7, 11, 19, 144
automobile accident on railroad tracks, 5
Avranche, 29

B

Baby Boomers, 135
barbed wire fences, 90
Barber, Frank, iii, x, xi, 4, 5, 153, 164
barges, 27, 89, 90, 102, 103
Bastogne, 77
Battle of the Bulge, vii, 59, 60, 70, 72, 77, 78, 81, 87, 92, 93, 119, 135, 147, 151, 154
beet fields, 52, 53, 54
Belgium, ix, 19, 39, 42, 44, 49, 50, 51, 52, 59, 61, 69, 70, 71, 76, 111, 146, 153, 163
Bergen Belsen, Germany, 115
bicycle, x, 1, 2, 3, 4, 5, 164
bicycle racing, gold medal, 3
bicycle racing, 1, 2, 3, 4, 163
bicycle, balloon tires, 1, 3
bicycle, BSA racing, 2

Index

bicycle, Schwinn, 1, 2
bicycle, stock, 1
bicycling, 1, 2, 5, 21, 163
boats, 4, 23, 27, 89, 99, 101, 102, 103, 118
Boston Harbor, 10, 14, 144, 153
Boston Port of Embarkation, 10, 144
Bradley, General Omar, 28, 29, 30, 31, 32, 34
Brest, 29, 145
bridges, 9, 56, 57, 74, 90, 99, 102, 112, 116, 118
British, 29, 31, 41, 43, 121, 131, 144
British troops, 121, 131
Brittany, 29, 30, 41
Brokaw, Tom, v
Brunswick, Germany, 113, 114, 123, 148, 155
Brussels, 51, 52
Buchenwald, 131, 137, 138, 139, 140, 149, 156
Buchenwald crematorium, 131
Buchenwald graveyards, 131
bunkers, 52, 53, 54, 55, 56, 57
Burgomeister, 113

C

Caen, 29, 31, 41
Camp Attebury, 10, 143
Camp Blanding, 7, 8, 9, 19, 143
Camp Forrest, 9, 19, 143
Camp Myles Standish, 10, 144
Canadian, 29, 31, 41, 144
chasing the Germans, 32, 35, 40, 42, 44
Cherbourg, 29, 30
Chicago, x, 1, 2, 3, 4, 5, 6, 134, 135, 143, 150, 163, 164
Chicago Pedal Pushers, 1
church steeple, 57
Cobra, 31, 33, 34, 41, 145
Columbus Park Wheelmen, 4, 163, 164
concentration camp, 115, 131
convoy, 10, 11, 144
Cotentin Peninsula, 29, 30
counterattack, 31, 32, 34, 39, 49, 71, 77
Coutance, 29
Csechoslovakian border, 131
cube of sugar, 52

D

Dachau Trials, 73
dancing girls, 59
D-Day, v, ix, 11, 19, 23, 144, 163
deceptive measures, 100
DeGaulle, General, 44
Detmold,. Germany, 112, 148
Dietrich, General Josef, 73
Division patches, 91, 100
Dorsten, Germany, 103, 105, 111, 148
Dubnick, John and Frank, 4, 5
dynamiting the Stavelot bridge, 75

E

Echt, Holland, 99, 147
Eiffel Tower, 44
Eisenhower, General, 31
Elbe River, 113, 114, 115, 116, 117, 123, 148, 155
Elgin to Chicago race, 2, 4
Engineering Battalion, 57
Engineering Corps, 90
England, vii, 11, 15, 19, 20, 21, 22, 23, 28, 31, 144, 151, 153
English aerial rocket attack, 32
English Channel, 19, 24, 27, 31, 50, 115, 134
English pubs, 21
English Typhoons, 35
Europe, v, ix, x, 7, 8, 19, 20, 32, 99, 104, 116, 118, 131, 135, 149, 163
evacuated Aachen, 58
Evreux, 43, 44, 146
extermination camp, 131

F

Falaise, 40, 42, 43, 49
Falaise Gap, 42, 148
Falaise Pocket or Trap, 40
false radio messages, 100
Farsleben, Germany, 114, 115
field maneuvers, 9, 143
First Army, 28, 29, 30, 31, 32, 33, 34, 41, 77, 145
flame throwers, 55, 56
flashlight, red baton, 5
Flers, 40
flood waters, 88, 93

Index

footbridges, 89
Fort Dix, 134
Fort Sheridan, 6, 7, 134, 143, 150
France, vii, ix, 19, 24, 29, 30, 31, 32, 34, 35, 39, 44, 49, 50, 51, 54, 69, 111, 134, 146, 150, 151, 163
Free French Army, 44
French coastal guns, 55
Fright, 104

G

Gahlen, Germany, 103, 104, 105, 148
Gaskill, Private, 51
Geneva Convention, 73
German High Command, 32, 35, 49, 104, 119, 146
German money, 117
German motorcycles, 93
German paratrooper school, 71
German SS Panzer, 73, 74, 75, 76, 104, 148
German submarine base, 29
German tri-motor transport plane, 71
Germany, v, ix, 19, 32, 35, 39, 41, 42, 44, 49, 50, 52, 53, 59, 62, 69, 72, 78, 93, 99, 105, 111, 115, 119, 123, 131, 132, 141, 142, 147, 148, 149, 150, 154, 155, 156, 163
girls panties, 21
Goering, 28
Gold Beach, 29
Great Depression, ix
Greatest Generation, v
Green Bay, 1
grenades, 55, 56
guard duties, 117

H

Hamelin, Germany, 111, 112, 113, 148
Hanover, Germany, 113
hedgerows, 8, 28, 30, 32
Heerlen, 52, 59, 69, 71, 87
Her Majesty's Household Cavalry, 43
Heydte, Friedrich von der, 72
Hill 314, 34
Hitler, 41, 71, 133
Hobbs, General, 113, 118
Holland, ix, 19, 44, 49, 50, 51, 69, 99, 111, 146, 147, 163

hospitals, 111
Humboldt Park Bike Racing Bowl, 3
Hunxe, Germany, 111, 112

I

Illinois-Michigan Canal, 1
Indiana, 10, 19, 143
Innsbruck, Austria, 133
invasion, v, 19, 22
Invasion, Allied, 28, 40
Irish Sea, 11

J

J.C. Pennie, 7
Japanese surrender, 135
Japanese War, 131
Jews, 115, 131
Joliet, Illinois, 1
Julich, 58, 59, 87, 88, 89, 91, 93, 99, 147
jumped off the train, 132
Juno Beach, 29

K

Kerkrade, 56, 57
KP duty, 7

L

LaGleize, 74, 75, 76
Lake Geneva, 4
Lake Michigan, 1
land mines, 53, 69, 90, 92
Landsberg Prison, 133
Landsberg, Germany, 132, 133, 134, 150
League of American Wheelmen (LAW), 2
LeHavre, 32, 150
Leine River, 113
LeMans, 41
liberated prisoners, 111
Liege, 52, 72, 73, 146
Liverpool, 11, 144
London, 11, 19, 20, 22, 144
looting, 116
Loviers, 44
Luftwaffe, 43
Lugers, 113

Index

M

Maas (Meuse) River, 99
Maastricht, 49, 50, 52, 147
machine guns, 30 and 50 caliber, 8, 32, 39, 51, 116
Magdeburg, 19, 39, 114, 115, 116, 117, 118, 119, 120, 121, 126, 127, 128, 131, 148, 149
Magdeburg, Germany, 19, 39, 114, 115, 116, 117, 118, 119, 120, 121, 126, 127, 128, 131, 148, 149
Malmedy, 70, 71, 72, 73, 74, 75, 76, 77, 79, 151, 154
Malmedy massacre, 73
Marienberg, 53, 54, 55
Marine, 101
Marlene Dietrich, 59
Massachusetts, 10, 144
massacred them, 73
McDonald, Charles B., 55
McNair, Lieutenant General Leslie, 34
ME109, 69
Mehrum, Germany, 100, 102
Mein Kampf, 133
messenger girls, 21
Meuse River, 52, 75, 146
military government, 116, 118, 149
military guard on trains, 132
Milwaukee, 1, 4
Missouri Ozarks, 5, 6, 153
Montagne, 43
Montgomery, Field General, 29, 30, 41, 42, 43
mopping up, 111, 112, 148
Mortain, vii, 30, 31, 32, 34, 35, 39, 40, 41, 49, 146, 151
Munich, Germany, 132, 133
Museum in London, 20, 76, 164
Muskegon, 1

N

Navy, 10, 101, 102, 164
Nazi concentration camp, 115, 131
New Jersey, 10
New York Harbor, 134, 150
Nonancourt, 43
Normandy, v, vii, ix, 8, 11, 23, 24, 27, 28, 29, 30, 31, 32, 35, 39, 41, 49, 50, 87, 144, 151, 163
Normandy Beach, ix, 11, 50, 163
Normandy beaches, v, 23, 29, 31, 50, 144
North Shore train, 134

O

Oak Park Cycle Club, 2, 4
Oak Park, Illinois, 1, 163
Oelsnitz, Germany, 131, 134, 141, 142, 149, 150, 156
Omaha Beach, vii, 19, 24, 27, 29, 32, 144, 151
Ork, Germany, 100, 101, 102, 103

P

Pacific War Theater, 102
PacificTheater, 131
pad of butter, 52
Panzer tanks, 75
paratroopers, 71, 72
Paris, vii, 41, 43, 44, 49, 146, 151
Patton, General, 31, 34, 41, 42, 144, 145
Peiper, Joachim, 73
Pied Piper of Hamelin, 112
pillboxes, 52, 54, 55, 56, 57
point system, 131, 134
prison camp, 73
prisoner of war camps, 119
prisoners, 40, 42, 51, 71, 73, 111, 115, 116, 119, 131, 132, 133
promoted to Pfc, 55

Q

Quartermasters, 112
Queen Mary, 134
Queen of Belgium, 52

R

radio, 33, 39, 43, 51, 100, 111
Radio, 33, 39, 43, 51, 100, 111
rafts, 89
rat-race, 111
Rayen, Germany, 99, 100, 147
Red Ball Express, 50
Regimental Engineers, 89
Rhine River, vii, 92, 93, 99, 148, 151
Richmond Golf Club, 22

Index

right and left traps, 40
Rockford, Illinois, 4
Roer River, vii, 58, 59, 69, 70, 71, 77, 78, 87, 88, 91, 93, 95, 99, 100, 147, 151, 154
Roer River upstream dams, 58
Rogatz, Germany, 114, 148
Roman Baths, 23
Russian Army, 19, 78, 119, 149
Russians, v, 19, 78, 114, 115, 116, 117, 118, 119, 124, 125, 126, 149, 155

S

Saint Lo, 30, 31, 32, 33, 34, 35, 39, 41, 49, 57, 76, 145
Salm River, 74
sand table, 56, 100
saturation bombing, 56, 89
Scared, 104
scattering for shelter, 69
Scherpenseel, 52, 53, 56, 57, 59
scopes, 8, 39, 51, 53, 54, 58, 74
Scrage, Seargent, 51
seafaring men, 23
Seine River, vii, 42, 43, 44, 49, 146, 151
showers, 69
Siegfried Line, vii, 49, 52, 53, 54, 55, 57, 58, 59, 62, 63, 69, 87, 92, 93, 135, 147, 151, 154
Silver Star, 55, 63, 154
Simpson, General, 101
Sittard, Holland, 99, 147
Smith, Dan, iii, iv, v, vii, xi, 6, 13, 15, 51, 54, 61, 62, 63, 79, 80, 95, 107, 123, 137, 141, 143, 153, 154, 155, 156, 163, 164
Smith, Mary Louise, 135, 163
Smith, Michael, xi
smoke, 90, 101, 103
smoke-bearing artillery shells, 90
Southampton, 23
Spa, 76
St. Barthelemy, 34, 35, 40
St. Lo all over again, 76
St. Vith, 76, 77
Statue of Liberty, 134, 150
Stavelot, 73, 74, 75, 76, 80, 154
Steinmetz High School, 1, 163
strategy planning, 91
students, 115

Stuka, 90, 92
submarines., 11
supplies, 8, 23, 27, 29, 32, 35, 39, 40, 49, 50, 53, 55, 59, 69, 74, 75, 77, 89, 92, 93, 103, 111, 112, 118
surrender, 29, 40, 112, 113, 116, 119, 135
surrendered Allied soldiers, 73
Sword Beach, 29

T

target bombing, 89, 102
Tea Time, 43
Tennessee, 8, 9, 10, 19, 93, 143
Teutoberger Wald, 112, 148
The Siegfried Line Campaign, 55
Third Army, 31, 32, 33, 34, 41, 42, 77, 145
Tournai, 52, 146
train crash, 132
training, 2, 3, 4, 7, 8, 9, 10, 20, 56, 93, 99, 100, 111, 143, 144
treadway bridges, 89
Trois Ponts, 74, 75
trolley cars, 116
trophy, 3, 4
trucks, 6, 10, 21, 27, 39, 50, 111, 118, 119, 120, 143
Tullahoma, 9

U

Ubach, 54, 57
undertaking, x, 1
upstream headwaters, 88
US Treasury, 118
Utah Beach, 29

V

Vire River, 33

W

Wales, 23
Wallach, Germany, 99, 100, 148
waterproof our jeeps, 23
Weimar, Germany, 131, 149
Wesel, 93, 99, 100, 101, 148
Weser River, 112

Index

West Wall, 49
whiskey, 76
Wiedman, Phyllis, 4
winter, 70
World War I, v, vii, ix, x, 4, 7, 72, 78, 104, 143, 151, 163, 164
World War II, v, vii, ix, x, 4, 7, 72, 78, 104, 143, 151, 163, 164
Wright Junior College, 1, 2, 7, 163

Wurm River, 52, 53, 56, 57

Y

Youth Hostel, 4, 5

Z

Zeiss scopes, 54

Author

Dan Smith was born in Oak Park, Illinois, a suburb of Chicago, in 1921. He graduated from Steinmetz High School in 1939 and then from Wright Junior College in 1941 with a Pre-Med degree. His early years were filled with bicycling - both racing and long-distance touring. In the early 1940's he was a member of a Chicago cycling club, the Columbus Park Wheelmen, when World War II broke out. He enlisted in the United States Army in September of 1942, and was assigned to serve in the 30th Old Hickory Infantry Division (Andrew Jackson's old Division). He was with the 30th Division during the D-Day landings on the Normandy Beaches in June of 1944 and then for the next year during the 30th Division's year-long combat battle drive eastward and northward through France, Belgium, Holland and Germany until the end of the war in Europe came when the Division had reached the vicinity of Berlin in Eastern German. The drive across Europe was a year-long period of unrelenting, day-to-day combat battle, and the many experiences that Dan had along the way are the subject of this book.

Dan and his wife, Mary Louise (who has passed away), were married for 64 years. Their family includes two sons, Michael and Robert, and three daughters, Margaret Mary Kelsey, Patricia Ann O'Hara, and Mary Louise Robles, and 15 grandchildren.

Co-Author

Frank Barber was born in Chicago, Illinois in 1920. He has a Bachelor of Science Degree from Northwestern University, Evanston, Illinois, and a Juris Doctor Degree from DePaul University School of Law, Chicago. After serving in the United States Navy during World War II, he went to work as an intellectual property attorney for  Armour and Company in Chicago. In 1971, Frank became Chief Patent and Trademark Counsel and moved with the Company to newly established headquarters in Phoenix, Arizona. After retiring in 1985, he has continued as a legal consultant for the Company (now The Dial Corporation) and has in addition developed a second career, specializing in computer databases. He also devotes considerable time and effort doing volunteer work on databases for the Phoenix Art Museum.

Frank and his wife, Betty, (who has passed away) were married for 52 years. Their family includes a son, John, and two daughters, Nancy Barber and Kathy Latham, and five grandchildren.

Frank Barber and Dan Smith have been good friends for over 70 years, starting with their bicycle riding days back in the early 1940's when they both belonged to the Columbus Park Wheelmen, a bicycle club in Chicago.